Edinburgh for Cyclists

**A GUIDE TO CYCLING
IN EDINBURGH AND LOTHIAN**

CREDITS

We'd like to thank the following people who made this book possible.

Publication Team Editors: Carol Crawford, Dave du Feu, Robert Smith.
Design: Ian Maxwell, Stewart Milne, Alun Thomas.

Contributers and other helper: David Bellos, Douglas Blair, Bill Clarke, Robin Cook, Peter Coutts, Kirsty Davidson, Sue Downie, Nick Evans, Patrick Gibb, Brian Gilmore, Dave Gordon, Richard Grant, John Hardie, Miles Horsey, Ian Hunter, Norman Ireland, Liz Leven, Chris Lindsay, Evan Lloyd, Chris Mackenzie, Alex Mann, Nick Marshall, Ken Moore, Norman Patterson, Linda Petzsch, Grazyna Portal, Bill Neilson, Ian Robertson, Dorothy Robinson, Cameron Rose, Susan Smith, Alison Spears, Anthony Strachan, Peter Teague, Edward Zoller.

Typists: Katherine Francis-Smith, Kathleen Jamie, Liz Turnbull, Agnes Wright, Ursula Johnson-Marshall.

Typesetting: Scottish Community Education Centre.

Graphics: Cartoons: Jerry Neville, Weef.

Freewheeling for allowing us the use of their office.

Finally we are very grateful to the Interim Secreteriat of Cycling Campaign Groups and local advertisers for making this venture financially possible.

First published: December 1980 (1200 copies)
Reprinted: June 1981 (1200 copies)

Published by SPOKES, 2 Ainslie Place, Edinburgh EH3 6AR. Tel: 225 6906.

FOREWORD

Over the past decade the bicycle has staged a dramatic recovery as a popular means of transport. Sales of new bicycles have risen steadily and now outnumber sales of vehicles by the ailing motor car industry.

It is not necessary to be a cycling fanatic to understand the origins of this trend. The bicycle is cheaper in both capital and running costs than the car and the cost advantage is certain to expand as the price of petrol rises. Cycling to work restores exercise as a matter of routine in a society which has eliminated exercise from the daily round to its own great peril. And in most urban environments, especially during the commuter rush hour, the bicycle is generally the fastest mode of transport.

Yet the resurgence of the bicycle remains remarkable because it has occurred at a time when transport policy and highway construction has been marked by an enthusiasm for the private car that would have won the admiration of Toad of Toad Hall. Those who remain reluctant to risk rush hour traffic by bike have rational grounds for their fears: many needless accidents occur as a result of our failure to consider the needs of cyclists, to maintain road surfaces near the kerb and to provide networks of cycle routes which would enable cyclists to avoid motorists and their attendant exhaust fumes. The flexibility of the bicycle is also constrained by the infrequency of secure parking facilities, and yet it is only within the last two years that highway authorities have been given the power to furnish cycle racks. The problem was succinctly expressed over a decade ago by a Minister of Transport. "There is a great future for the bicycle if you make conditions right. If you make them wrong there isn't any future."

Spokes is an organisation which has acquired considerable battle honours in getting conditions made right for cyclists. In a short period of existence they have obtained commitment to half a dozen cycleways in Edinburgh and the first contra-flow cycle lane in the city. These would not have been secured without the careful preparation and persistent pressures supplied by Spokes. I commend their book as an invaluable handbook for the city cyclist.

Robin Cook, MP
10th September 1980

Robin Cook (Centre) at SPOKES 1980 May Rally.

Contents

1 Cycling in Edinburgh

Edinburgh Evening News

Mr. Edward Zoller.

**THE HISTORY OF CYCLING IN
EDINBURGH AND LOTHIAN
by Edward Zoller, President,
Lothians District Association of the
Cyclists' Touring Club.**

Relatively few of our citizens realise how closely the city has been associated with
the growth of cycling since the days of the Ordinary or "High Bicycle".

With the growing interest in both the Ordinary, and its competitor the tricycle, in
the early 1870s, it was inevitable that kindred spirits would get together, and so it was
in March 1870 that the Edinburgh Amateur Bicycle Club was constituted as the world's
first cycling club, although this claim has been disputed ever since by the London based
Pickwick Bicycle Club. Edinburgh can certainly claim to have been in at the start of a
movement which, with periodic ups and downs, has thrived and spread around the
globe. Regrettably, the EABC appears to have faded away towards the end of the 1930s
through failure to recruit new young blood. A move in 1927 to absorb the Lothians
Cycling Club (a young racing club — not to be confused with the Lothians District
Association of the CTC, although a number of riders belonged to both clubs) — came to
naught when, I understand, several older EABC members objected that the proposed
merger contravened the rules of the EABC. It was a pity to see the old name die out.

A volume of "Cycling" covering the period August 1879 to July 1881 in the
writer's possession lists six other Edinburgh clubs founded in the 70s, including the
Edinburgh University Cycling Club.

While local clubs were growing in numbers during these years there was no national
organisation for the collection and exchange of information on road conditions and the
like. Remember that the development of the railways had lead to the neglect of roads
for distance travel. There had been correspondence in the national cycling press of the
time regarding the need for some form of national body to look after the interests of
the growing number of touring cyclists, provide for the exchange of information, put
prospective tourists in touch with one another and "so facilitate the association of
companionable men" as one writer put it.

FOUNDING OF THE CTC

At this stage enter Stanley J. Cotterell, who was a young medical student at Edinburgh University and already a member of the Midlothian BC. A keen tourist, he became so absorbed with the idea of a "Touring Club" that he seems to have neglected his studies to write to the Press and Cycling clubs all round the country "plugging" his ideas. He aroused sufficient interest and promises of support for a meeting to be arranged at the Annual Cyclists' Bank Holiday meet at Harrogate in August 1878. So Cotterell set off on his Ordinary from his student "digs" at 1 Moncrieff Terrace and rode to Harrogate, where on 5th August a meeting was held and it was agreed to form the Bicycle Touring Club as it was first called. In these days perhaps the gentlemen on their high wheels rather looked down on the "eccentric" types who would insist on riding on three wheels, and did not wish to include them in the new Touring Club. Whatever the reason, the title was changed to the Cyclists' Touring Club in 1882. Thus, Edinburgh has a strong interest in the formation of the world's first "Touring Club", which became the pattern for other Touring Clubs around the world, and indeed, later, motoring clubs.

Cycling was booming all over the country and reached a peak in the late 90s. In Edinburgh Six Day races held in the Waverley Market seem to have attracted the crowds. A recent 'Scotsman' quote of 100 years ago recorded that a week long race in the "Market" had attracted some 100,000 spectators. These would be professional events. For the amateur club enthusiasts races were held on the roads, mainly on a handicap basis to provide, in theory at least, a mass finish. Although frowned upon by authority and harried by police on occasion, there were times when the local bobby was an interested spectator, and I have been told of a Scottish 25 mile championship race not far from Edinburgh where the local policeman appeared at the start to say that he had seen to it that all dogs at farms along the course had been locked up in case they chased any of the competitors!

LOCAL TRADERS

For a number of years towards the end of the century the local cycle dealers arranged an annual cycle show in the Waverley Market and judging from the catalogue, the hall must have been well filled. With the development of motorcycles, they and cars began to appear at the show. It may interest readers that several well known local firms started in the cycle trade before getting caught up with the "newfangled" motorised vehicles. Ross and Sleigh were postal workers who started to sell bicycles from a shop at Goldenacre and later developed into Rossleigh Ltd. "Old J.R." Alexander and his racing sons also gravitated to motorcycles and the famous Model T Ford and the family name lives on today. One business which has stayed faithful to its founders cycling enthusiasm still bears his name in Churchill — Tom Piper. Edinburgh clubs had, I think, two members riding for the Scottish team which took part in the Olympic Games Road Race in Sweden in 1912.

The 1914-18 War almost literally wiped out the clubs which had been active during these early years of the century, but with a number of more elderly members, the Lothians DA CTC was able to survive in a restricted way. Two teenagers joined early in 1920, became fired with enthusiasm for the freedom of the open road and started the long, slow battle to build up the Club again. In 1923 the Cycle Trade association decided to organise a National Bicycle Week to publicise and boost interest in cycling. The CTC and the now defunct IOGT Cycling Club, as the only two clubs then functioning in the town, were very much involved with a local committee of cycle dealers in the planning of the "Week's" programme and eventually leading the rides each evening and at the weekend in and around Edinburgh. These rides attracted several hundred riders each evening and more on the Saturday when there was a competition for two cycles presented by traders. The "Week" received and generated very wide publicity and undoubtedly helped to increase interest in the local clubs.

BETWEEN THE WARS

By the time a number of the younger riders in the CTC were showing an interest in competition and as a result of contacts established during NBW with Tom Piper and Norman Ireland, who had been racing in the immediate pre-1914 War era, and a number of other "more energetic" riders, it was decided to form a racing club. The Lothians CC was started in 1924 and two years later the Edinburgh Road Club was started as a racing off-shoot of the CTC. There followed a long period of interclub rivalry, particularly in the field of distance and place to place records authenticated by the Road Records Association of Scotland. Between them these two clubs have established fifty-five RRA of S records and in addition five British National RRA records.

When the Scottish Youth Hostels Association was formed local cyclists took a very active part in its development. There was a time when cyclists and walkers predominated in the hostels!

During the mid 1930s club cycling in Edinburgh reached a peak and I am indebted to George Kay, who as "Clubman" edited the cycling column in the Evening News. The column was based on a list of 95 cycling clubs in and around Edinburgh, who submitted their fixture lists for his weekly column.

As with 1914, 1939 saw the beginning of the end for these, mostly small, clubs, and to the best of my knowledge only four on that list are functioning today. Since the war several others have, however, been formed.

SPOKES entry '100 years of Cycling' in the 1980 Festival Cavalcade.

CHARITY EVENTS

Organised cyclists have always been ready to assist with charity collections since the days when the Ordinary and Tricycle clubs paraded in their uniforms in aid of collections for Boer War widows. The Edinburgh Room at the Central Library has a number of photographs of these early parades. When the Evening News was sponsoring its "Shilling Fund" in aid of the Royal Infirmary there were, for a number of years, well supported fancy dress parades with street collections. These parades were headed by a cycling contingent, to enable them to ride clear of the walkers and floats, with a number of riders on historic machines — Ordinaries, a Michaux Boneshaker, Coventry Rotary and other tricycles, a lady front tandem tricycle and a four wheeled tandem! In aid of the same Fund, local clubs joined forces for joint Cyclists Dances at the Palais de Dance in Fountainbridge. Exclusively booked for the Clubs, attendances over a period of years varied from around 300 to 600. As a commentary on costs then and now, the 2/6d (12½p) admission ticket covered also a waitress service of coffee and biscuits once during the evening, and at that figure a handsome profit was made for the Fund!

During the last war travel and other restrictions prevented many people from getting away on holiday, so the Edinburgh Corporation asked recreational organisations to help by organising activities for "Holidays at Home". With the demise of most of the small clubs, it again fell to the CTC to provide organisation and leadership for evening and weekend rides during the summer months. These were well supported by local riders, many of whom had never even explored their own town, far less the surrounding country, and they were delighted to be guided around, see properties not normally open to the public, and such unusual sights as the oil well then in production at D'Arcy. Now with the threatened drying up of supplies, and the cost of the stuff, more and more people are coming to realise that the bicycle — which prophets of doom for most of the last 100 years have been assuring us to be dead — is very much alive to provide not only convenient transport, but healthy recreation for all ages, and an "open sesame", both to our local landscape and to that wonderful country which is Scotland.

Further information about the CTC can be found in Appendix 1.

BIKE IT
By SPOKES Resources Group

REASONS FOR CYCLING

Bicycles can be used for day-to-day commuting, for leisure, and for sport. Why cycle? As well as being the cheapest, most efficient, non-polluting form of personal transport it has many other advantages both for the individual and the community. These benefits are:-

FOR THE COMMUNITY

Reduces congestion — bikes take little space, moving or parked.
Quietness
Safety for other travellers — especially for pedestrians.
Saves energy — bikes take less energy to make or to run than other forms of transport.
Cleanliness — no fumes or exhausts, no lead or carbon monoxide.
Cheap — locking facilities and cycle tracks are very cheap.

FOR THE INDIVIDUAL

Healthy — but you needn't be an athlete to cycle regularly to work.
Cheap — cheap to buy and run compared to motor transport.
Safe — if proper facilities are provided.
Fast in towns — average speed equal to cars.
Door-to-door travel — no changing or looking for parking places.
Social — cyclists can say "hello" at traffic lights.
Maintenance is quick and simple — few tools are needed.
Getting to know the city — using back streets will lead to all sorts of discoveries.

GO TO WORK ON A BIKE

BUYING A BIKE
NEW

**Buy a new bike only from a specialist shop who will give it a thorough pre-sale check, provide spares and after-sales service, advise you on the most suitable model for your needs, and adapt the bike to your requirements; e.g. fitting a low gear or adding shopping pannier bags.

**If you are buying a second-hand bike make sure that it is the correct size — a rough check is that you should be able to straddle the frame comfortably with your feet flat on the ground. If you can't check the bike mechanically yourself take along someone who can.

**What kind of bike you should buy depends partly on how far you intend to cycle. Large-wheel bikes are the most efficient and adaptable, although for short or medium distances small-wheel or folding bikes are fine.

**Since Edinburgh is hilly, gears are advisable. Hub gears (Sturmey Archer) are extremely reliable but give less range than derailleur gears. What is important is not the number of gears but that there is a sufficiently wide ratio between them. If you decide to get derailleur gears it is worth asking for the largest sprocket on the rear wheel to be at least 32 or 34 teeth, so that you have a very low gear.

A SPOKES survey of all the major cycle shops in Edinburgh and Lothian appears after this section.

SECOND-HAND

Give any bikes a thorough check mechanically. Watch for bent forks, buckled wheels, worn brakes and rust in strategic places etc. Check it is the correct size and that the seller really does own the bike *before buying it.*

One way to avoid trouble is to buy a used bike from a bike shop where it will be throughly checked before leaving the shop.

*See survey to find out which shops recondition bikes.

Other sources are police auctions, jumble sales and the Bicycles Columns in both the Scotsman (column 063) and the Evening News (column 063).

CARRYING

Many types of conveyance are available.

1.   Your **back** — a small rucksack or shoulder bag with strap long enough to go diagonally across your shoulders, are best. **Do not try to carry anything heavy on your back** it is inefficient and dangerous.
2.   **Basket** — Best for bikes with flat handlebars and ideal for shopping. However with larger weights, baskets without separate brackets tend to rub down on front mudguard and impede the front wheel.

3.   Conventional **saddlebag** — useful for **small** items e.g. tools, locks and keys.
4.   **Backcarrier** — this can be fitted with rubber strap with hooks, and panniers. **Panniers** are convenient, **versatile** and roomy — once you have used them you are unlikely to go back to other methods. The best designs easily lift on and off and though initial outlay is great they can be used for touring too.
5.   **Trailers** — Some recent designs are stable and are suitable for carrying the largest items around town — one maker claims a washing machine can be transported!

KEEPING YOUR BIKE

**Buy a proper lock and chain and use it all the time, locking the frame of the bicycle to railings, etc. in the street. Most good bike shops can supply "case hardened" chains and padlocks; or you can buy a padlock and length of chain (e.g. at McLarens in Bread Street) and insert this in a length of old inner tube to protect the bikes from scratches. Remember it only takes a few seconds for a thief to hop on an unlocked bike and ride off; and bikes have a very good second hand value.

**Keep a note of the frame number which is usually under the bottom bracket, between the pedals. Police stations will supply you with a free record card to keep a note of details of your bike in case it gets stolen.

**Get your bike insured. Some dealers will arrange this or it can be done through the Cyclists Touring Club if you are a member. But check your house insurance policy — your bike may already be covered and if not you can probably include it for a small additional premium. See below.

INSURANCE

Insurance is a necessity in case of theft or accident. The Theft Group is preparing a consumer report on Insurance companies carried out on a national scale with the help of 'Freewheeling' magazine to find out how insurance companies differ in their treatment of actual claims as well as the difference between their policies and premiums. This should be ready in late 1980.

In the meantime the options are as follows:

1.   *Cyclebag* the Bristol cycle group have an insurance scheme which has now been extended to all members of all groups within the Interim Secretariat of Cycle Campaign Groups. Contact Spokes Theft Group for details.
2.   *Bike Shops* — Even if you did not buy your bike from the shop many shops offer insurance on all bikes and the rates seem reasonable. Check survey for details.
3.   Join a *cycling club* with special insurance policies for members for example the C.T.C. or the B.C.F.

4. If you have a *house insurance* policy you can normally insure a bike for an additional payment. There are many Insurance companies listed in the Yellow Pages but very few will now take bikes alone. One company which does offer a policy for non-house holders is Endsleigh (Bristo Street), but you must insure your other personal belongings at the same time.

Finally *ensure that you know the full policy terms.* Check that the bike is insured away from the house if it is insured with the house. Find out if it is insured with the replacement or actual value of the bike and whether there is a cash limit on a claim.

SAFETY

Cyclists are more vulnerable than motorists. On the other hand they are higher, have unimpeded vision all round and can hear better. Take advantage of this and **be aware of what is going on around you. Watch out especially for motorists who carelessly open car doors. Pedestrians occasionally will not see you — they expect to hear a vehicle. Choose a quiet route to get from A to B if possible instead of the busy one the cars use. Have proper lights and wear bright clothing. Use a bell.

It is important that your **brakes work well in **dry and wet** weather. Careful adjustment is essential. If your wheel rims are made of alloy you get much better braking in the wet than if they are steel or chrome. You can buy special wet-weather leather Fibrax brake blocks which grip steel rims better than rubber blocks do — but they are more expensive and wear out relatively quickly.

As regards safe routes read Chapter 5, 'Spokesways', which explains what SPOKES Network Group have been doing. For further hints about safe cycling read Chapter 3 composed by SPOKES Safety Group which includes what to do in an accident.

CYCLE CLIPS — are advisable especially if the bike doesn't have a chain guard and you wear the more flapping styles of trousers. Metal ones or those made of reflective material are best.

LIGHTS AND REFLECTORS

For night cycling you must by law have a rear reflector and front and rear lights. At present all lighting systems on the market have serious drawbacks, but there is a lot of development going on in this field.

1. *Battery lights* — These are cheap to buy but expensive to run. They also tend to get stolen.
2. *Dynamo lights* — These are more expensive to buy but cost nothing to run. They are much less likely to get stolen but go out when you stop (e.g. at traffic lights). There are three main types. The *hub dynamo* is relatively expensive and is built-in on a wheel hub. The *rim dynamo,* which runs off the side of the tyre is cheaper but has disadvantages. It can slip in the wet, it can chew a groove in the tyre, and it is more work to pedal. A recent development is the *Sanyo Dynapower* which runs from the tread of the tyre and overcomes all the problems of the *rim dynamo.*

3. *Further developments* — Many new systems are beginning to come onto the market. There are battery-assisted dynamos, to keep you alight at traffic lights. Some of these are rechargeable. There are also complete rechargeable lighting sets and there is even a new rechargeable quick-release lighting system (to overcome theft problems) which for convenience packs entirely into a plastic tub which fits into a bicycle water-bottle carrier!

MAINTENANCE AND REPAIRS

If your bike is new there is consumer protection legislation which applies to damage resulting from defects in manufacture or assembly. The manufacturers guarantee usually extends for between 6 months and a year. During this period the shop will either repair the bike themselves or send it back to the manufacturer. See SPOKES survey for details of the after sales service available in Edinburgh bike shops.

If your bike is in the more 'mature' bracket there are a number of options:

1. *Do-it-yourself* using maintenance manuals.
**Particularly recommended are: *Richards Bicycle Book* by R. Ballantine — a comprehensive and entertaining guide to choosing, using and maintaining your bike.
**Reader's Digest Basic Guide to the Maintenance of Bicycles — good for basic tasks.
See 'Books for the cyclist' for more details of each of these.
2. If you have difficulties following the technicalities in the manuals or lack the tools to do certain repairs. Free use of tools and expert help and advice are available from The Friends of the Earth Community Bicycle Workshop, 27 Drummond Street, Sundays, 7-9 pm.
3. Take your bike into your *local bike shop* or one of the *specialist repair centres* listed below.
There is debate about which are the best repair items to carry with you in everyday cycling. You may find the following useful — puncture repair kit, dumbell spanner, levers, and a pump. Some would advocate carrying a spare inner tube which takes little space and may save time. (Puncture can be located later in the comfort of your home). For longer distances, take spare bulbs, batteries, brake blocks, screwdriver, cycle oil, spoke key, pliers and possibly a small adjustable spanner.

CLOTHING

Finally *weather.* Cycling makes you more aware of our weather and of the need to carry special clothing in case it changes.

On *sunny* days it can be glorious; there is no better way of travelling around Edinburgh.

On *rainy* days you needn't be miserable with a cycling cape or waterproof trousers and jacket. Believe it or not Edinburgh has a very low rainfall (26") compared to some parts of the country, because it is on the east coast.

On *wintery* mornings cycling will keep you warm as you whizz past shivering, stomping bus-queues. The best advice is to wear a wooly hat; you will find if your head is warm the rest of you feels warm too!

BIKE SHOP SURVEY
By Carol Crawford of SPOKES Resources Group

In the early summer of 1980 a survey was made of all the major bike shops in Edinburgh and Lothian. A questionnaire was taken to each shop and a number of questions, designed to find out the services available, were asked of the owner/manager. Their responses are summarised in the following tables; Table I shows dealers for new bikes and Table 2 shows shops whose main business is to recondition bikes and repairs.

First it is necessary to explain what the questions were, why we asked them and what can be deduced from the responses. Only one shop (McCracken of Davidson's Mains garage) refused to answer our questions. A few shops were not visited — mainly secondhand shops, which are listed in the Yellow Pages, and two branches of Halfords which it was deemed would be similar to the shop in Hanover Street.

EXPLANATION OF MAIN TABLE

Columns 1 — 3	Designed to aid you in locating the bike shop.
Column 4	The date on which the shop was founded. As you will see 7 shops opened during 1980. These may lag behind the others in terms of experience but all seemed very enthusiastic and keen to help the cyclist.
Columns 5 — 6	Intended to give some idea of the relative size of the shop. For Column 5 we asked for the number of bikes in stock at that point in time. For Column 6 we asked the number of bike firms a shop dealt with. In some cases where a larger manufacturer has taken over a smaller one, the latter still seems to be considered as having a separate range: for example, Raleigh and Carlton. Where this is the case, they are counted here as 2 ranges. A shop with a larger number of ranges and bikes obviously has greater browsing potential.
Column 7	Indicates which makes are stocked. This helps if the potential customer wants to look at a specific make he/she may have heard about. At least 35 makes of new bike are to be found in Edinburgh shops.
Column 8	Describes any usual bikes. We asked specifically about tandems, unicycles and tricycles and then asked if their were any others they would *like* to mention.
Column 9	Though the main shops which recondition bikes have been separated into Table 2, many of the new bike dealers also deal with secondhand bikes, but some will only take them as a trade-in on a new bike.
Column 10	An indication of the range of attachments available in each shop. We asked which of the following 8 items were stocked; trailers, child or animal seats, panniers, baskets, specialised clothing (meaning wet weather or safety clothing), helmets and spacer flags, and also whether they wished to mention anything else.

Column 11a	Shows the guarantee period during which bikes can be taken back and repaired free if anything goes wrong due to a flaw in construction. Some shops were unable to give an exact length saying that it varied or that it depended on the manufacturer's guarantee period. The manufacturer usually guarantees a bike for 6 months or 1 year but frames and forks are normally guaranteed longer; 5-10 years. Other shops put their own guarantee on top of this.
Column 11b	Shows whether the shop offers a free check-up on a new bike after the customer has been using it for a few weeks or months to check everything is correctly adjusted so as to be running as it should. The period after which the customer should bring the bike in is also shown. In some shops, for example some newly opened ones this was not yet shop practice but the owner thought it a good idea. They either gave an estimated period or stated that they would be willing to look over a bike bought from the shop if the customer 'just brought it in'.
	In many cases it will be necessary for you to ask for this check-up. Finally some shops felt that they checked the bike fully before it left the shop and that a further check was unnecessary although most were willing to look at a bike if the customer requested it. SPOKES considers the free *check-up* to be a desirable piece of after sales service and hopes it will become automatic.
Column 12	Indicates whether the shop carried out repairs and if there are any restrictions on what they repair. Most shops do do repairs but in some shops or with certain repairs the bike may be returned to the manufacturer (e.g. Halfords) or sent to a specialist which takes longer. The main restriction appears to be availability of parts, generally most British bikes can be repaired. Space may also be limiting.
	Timing: Many shops especially the more central ones are likely to take longer to do repairs in summer than in winter owing to the 'pressure of work'. Other busy times are before public holidays or during school holidays. Out of town shops are more likely to be able to give an accurate prediction of how long a repair will take; normally 1-3 days. For the shops in Table 2 we have been able to give an indication of timing.
Column 13	Shows whether the shop offers insurance against accident or theft on (a) bikes purchased there and (b) on any bike. Where the answer to (b) is 'yes' note that some of these shops will only insure the newer bikes.

In the second Table exactly the same questions were asked and symbols and abbreviations used are the same throughout. However less sections are applicable.

A final word: The cycle trade in Edinburgh and Lothian seems to be on the increase with the opening of 7 new shops in 1980. But this can by no means be considered a final table: the 25 bike shops named here are only 1 more than the number in Leith alone during cycling's earlier heyday!

HIRING BIKES

3 Lothian shops hire out bikes:

Wheels: of Haddington have 2 bikes for hire.

Cycles of West Preston Street have 10 bikes for hire.

Edinburgh Cycle Hire 9 Alvanley Terrace, Whitehouse Loan Tel: 228 6363 gave us a few more details. Part of the 'Recycles' Co-operative, the hire section was begun in 1978. They have 90 bikes in all: 3 Speeds (Raleigh and Elswick Hopper). Ladies 5 Speeds (Crown) and Gents 10 Speeds (Raleigh, Falcon   Black Diamond). *Panniers* may also be hired.

Point of interest. At the end of each season the hire fleet is sold for two-third—three-quarter of new price depending on wear and tear. Before this all bikes are mechanically overhauled and each bike carries a 6 month guarantee.

Finally 2 shops *Pedal Power* of Gorgie Road and *Robin Williamson* intend to hire out bikes from summer 1981.

ABBREVIATIONS USED

TABLE 1

Column 4 F. Date — Founding date

Column 7 Bike makes avaialble

A — Annabella
A1 — Alan
Ben — Benotto
Bic — Bickerton
BJ — Bob Jackson
CE — Coventry Eagle
Col — Colnago
Cro — Crown
D — Dawes
EH — Elswick Hopper
F — Falcon
Gra — Graziella
H — Holdsworthy
HCB — Holdsworthy including Claud Butler (2)
HFG — Holdsworthy including Freddie Grubb (2)
JT — Jack Taylor
K — Kalkhoff
OM — Own Make
Mar — Marlborough
MKM — MKM
Mer — Mercian
M — Moorlands
MGt — Moorlands including Gitane (2)
Mot — Motobecane
Pas — Pashley
Pan — Pannonia
Peu — Peugeot
Puc — Puch
R — Raleigh
Rca — Raleigh including Carlton (2)
Rat — Rattrays
Vik — Viking
Vin — Vindec
Vis — Trusty — Viscount
W — Witcomb
+ — **Stock Frames**

Column 8 Unusual Bikes

Ord — Can be ordered (not in Stock)
Tan — Tandem
Tri — Tricycle
U — Unicycle
EB — Exercise Bike
BMX — Bicycle Motocross
Trip — Triplet
L — Specialist Lightweight Bikes
STB — Specialist Touring Bikes
Del — Delivery Bikes

Column 9 — Rec? Do you Recondition Bikes? 2nd hand? Do you deal with 2nd hand bikes?
(T) — Only as a Trade-in
Occ- Occasionally

Column 10 Attachments available
B — Baskets
CS — Child or animal seats
H — Helmets
P — Panniers
SC — Specialised Clothing
SF — Spacer Flags
T — Trailers
(X)   Other:
(1)   Safety vests
(2)   Other safety gadgets
(3)   Lightweight and towing items
(4)   Footwear and specialist lighting
(5)   Range of locks and lights
(6)   Full range of parts

Column 11 After Sales Service
11a GP — Length of Guarantee Period

$\leqslant$ up to   * as long as orignal owner retains
    2nd — even on 2nd hand bikes

11b Free check — Do you do a free check-up? — if so how long?

Manuf — Manufacturers guarantee period
Varies — Depends on fault, use, and length of
        manufactures guarantee period
ACR — At customer's request
X — Felt to be unnecessary if bike is fully
        checked before leaving shop
CC — Cotterless chainset checked after 150 miles
$\geqslant$ — greater than or equal too

Column 12 Repairs
With parts — Provided parts required for
        repair are available
Not Ital — Does not have parts to repair Italian
        bikes
Own first — Would repair cycles sold from shop
        first, then others if work in hand is not too
        great
Own bikes — Only repair bikes sold there
Not frames — Not frame repairs

TABLE 2

Columns 1—4 as Table 1
Column 6 See column 8 of Table 1
Column 7 as Column 10 of Table 1. 2nd—2nd hand
Column 8 as Column 11 of Table 1
Column 9 as Column 12 of Table 1

TABLE I NEW BIKE DEALERS

1. AREA	2. NAME PHONE NO.	3. ADDRESS	4. F. DATE	5. NO. BIKES	6. NO. MAKES	7. NAMES OF MAKES
E. LOTHIAN Bathgate	J. Anthony Armadale 30265	115 South St, Armadale Bathgate.	1945	300	8+	D,EH,F,HCB Puc,R,etc. +
MIDLOTHIAN Penicuik	Baird Cycle Centre Penicuik 72947	The Angle Park Garage John St, Penicuik.	1950	200	6	R etc
Dalkeith	Kean Sport 663-1859	130-136 High St. Dalkeith. (2 Shops)	1974 1980	120	8	EH,F,K,Pas, Peu,Puc,RCa
E. LOTHIAN Haddington	Wheels Haddington 3234	69 Market St. Haddington	1928	20	3	EH,R,Vin
Musselburgh	E. A. Peterson 665-2006 or 2530	35-39 High St. Musselburgh	1945	180	7	D,EH,F,Puc, R,Vin,Vis
EDINBURGH Corstorphine	Lawries Toys & Cycles 334-6216	115-117 St. Jonn's Rd. Corstorphine	1964	300	5	EH,Puc,RCa Vin
Gorgie	Pedal Power 337 1753	171 Gorgie Rd.	1980	50	3	Puc,R,Vik
Slateford	City Cycles 337 2351	87 Slateford Rd.	1980	30-50	4	Pan,Mar,M, Vin
Tollcross	Macdonald's Cycle Centre 229 8473	26-28 Morrison St.	1937	800	12	Al,Bic,D,E,HCB, + Mot,Peu,Pas,Puc,RCa
Bruntsfield	Recycles 228 1368	5-6 Alvaney Ter. Whitehouse Loan	1980	200	12	B.J,Cro,E,F,HCB,FG, + Mer,MKM,Mot,Pas,RCa,Vin
Churchill	Thomas Piper 447 1040	41 Morningside Rd.	1895	209	8	D,EH,F,HGB,Puc RCa
Morningside	Robin Williamson Cycles 447 4383	105 Comiston Rd. (New shop 26 Hamilton Pl)	1978 1980	60	14	CE,D,EH,F,HCB,Mot,Pas Puc,RCa,Vin,Vis,W +
Newington	Cycles 667 6239	12 West Preston St.	1920	300	13+	Bic,D,EH,F,H,JT,MGt, Pas,Puc,R,Rat,Vik,Vin etc.
Central	Halfords 226 3562	14 Hanover St. (2 other shops)	1927	150	2	OM,R
Stockbridge	Raeburn Cycle Centre —	63 Raeburn Place	1980	50-60	4	Mar,R,Vin, etc.
Leith	Sandy Gilchrist Cycles 554 2509	145 Restalrig Rd.	1970	300-400	14	A,Ben,Bic,Col,D,E,F, MGt,Peu,Puc,Vin,Vis,Vik

1 Has Raleigh mechanics certificate, but no time now to recondition bikes for shop is always busy. Still builds wheels.

2 Also car and motorcycle garage.

3 The new shop is devoted entirely to new cycles and accessories. Hire purchase available.

4 Can order any British Bike. 'Reliable and responsible shop'. Space small so early collection of repairs appreciated. Hiring.

5 'Service on cycles sold by us guaranteed at all times regardless of how long owner retains bike'.

6 Can order most bikes, Hire purchase available, Christmas Club, Hiring from summer 1981. 'Excellent and friendly service'.

7 Cycling family, chose Slateford because of lack of shops there then (Easter 1980). Friendly and helpful service and advice.

8 Pre-Xmas rush for repairs.

TABLE II 2nd HAND BIKES, RECONDITIONING AND REPAIR CENTRES

1. AREA	2. NAME PHONE NO.	3. ADDRESS	4. F. DATE	5. BIKES AVAILABLE	6. UNUSUAL BIKES
Portobello	Smith's Cycles	32 High St. Portobello	1930	Can order any new bike.	Can order
Leith	J. B. Allan 554 6698	14/16 Jane St.	c 1900	Can do almost anything, building and reconditioning. Can order new bikes.	Builds Tri, U. and Tan (including Tandems for blind) Specialises in bikes for 3-5 year olds.
Leith	Pedal Power 554 7143	33 Iona St.	1979	50 2nd Hand Bikes +20 waiting to be reconditioned at any time. Whole range.	Occasionally get tandems and Tricycles. Supply V. variable.
Newington	Recycles Repair Centre 667 2556	3 West Crosscauseway	1977	Deal with 2nd Hand Bikes and recondition bikes.	Chiefly a repair centre. Builds wheels.

14

8. UNUSUAL BIKES	9. REC. 2nd HAND	10. ATTACH-MENTS	11. AFTER SALES G.P.	Free Check	12. REPAIRS RESTRICTIONS	13. INSURANCE OWN BIKES?	ANY BIKE?	14. COMMENTS
Tan,U,Tri, (all ord.)	No / Yes(T)	B,CS,H,P SC,SF	Manuf	Yes varies	Yes with parts	Yes	Yes	1
—	No / Yes(T)	B,P.	Varies	Yes ACR	No	No	No	2
Tri,	Yes / Yes	B,CS,H,P SC,SF,T.	6 months	No	Yes / No	Yes	Yes	3
—	Yes / Yes	B,CS,P, SF.	1 yr. +2nd	Yes ≤1 yr.	Yes not Ital.	No	No	4
—	No / No	B,CS,P,	6 months	No	Yes / No	Yes	Yes	
Tan,Tri.	Yes / No	B,CS,P, SF.	*!	Yes 2 wks	Yes own first	Yes	Yes	5
BMX	No / Yes(T)	B,CS,H,P SC,SF (1)	≥6 months	Yes ACR	Yes with parts	Yes	No	6
Tan,U, Trip(ord).	No / Yes	B,CS,H, P,SC,SF.	Varies	Yes 1-4 wks	Yes / No	Yes	No	7
Tan,U,Tri, Del(ord),BMX	Yes / Yes	B,CS,H, P,SC,SF.	Varies	Yes 6 months	Yes with parts	Yes	Yes	8
Tan,Tri, STB.	No / No	B,CS,H,P, SC,SF,T (2)	Manuf	Yes 4-6 wks	Yes own bikes	No	No	9
Tri.	No / Yes	B,CS,P, SC,SF,T.	Manuf	No X,CC	Yes / No	Yes	Yes	10
U,Tan(ord) Tri(ord),BMX	Occ. / Occ.	B,CS,H,P, SC,SF,T (3)	1 yr.	Yes 4 wks	Yes not frames	Yes	Yes	11
Tan,U,Tri.	Yes / Yes	B,CS,H P,SC,SF	1 month	Yes 6 months	Yes / No	Yes	Yes	12
Tan,Tri EB,BMX	No / No	B,CS,H, P,SC,SF,T	1 yr.	Yes ≤1 yr.	Yes own bikes	Yes	No	13
—	Yes / Yes(T)	B,SC,P SF	1 day	No	Yes / No	No	No	14
U, L.	Yes / Yes	B,CS,H P,SC,SF (4)	1 yr.	Yes ACR	Yes / No	Yes	Yes	15

9   Friendly shop where people can leisurely browse and receive expert advice. Part of Recycles Co-op with repair and hire centres.

10   'Book in' system for repairs at busy times. Insurance on bikes not bought there depends on condition of cycle.

11   Most repairs done same day except when busy. Hope to hire in 1981 Advice on all aspects of cycling. New shop opening October 1980.

12   All year round repairs. Hires out bikes.

13   +2000 bikes in warehouse. Will do odd repair if there is time. Other shops: 138 Lothian Road (Tollcross) 67-73 Gt. Junction St. (Leith)

14   Repairs normally take less than 1 week.

15   Specialise in wheel building. Will alter any bike to customers requirements.

7. ATTACH-MENTS	8. AFTER SALES G.P.	Free Check	9. REPAIRS? RESTRICTIONS/TIMING		10. COMMENTS
B,CS,P (all ord.)	Manuf	Yes ACR	Yes / No	2 days for most	Business is to undertake any cycle repair. Cycle sales secondary.
B,CS,H, P,SC (6)	1 yr.	Yes (never had to ACR. X	Yes / No	1 wk – 10 days	Qualified bike mechanic. Builds bikes to customers specification and does awkward repairs for most other shops in town.
B,CS(2nd) P,SC	2 wks	Yes ACR X	Yes with parts	Quick	Will work long hours to finish work in hand. Business is in mechanically sound 2nd Hand bikes.
B,CS,P, SC,SF (5)(3)	6 mths	Yes 1 month	Yes with parts	1-2 wks	Specialise in repairing 'working bikes'. Have tools and parts to do all kinds of repairs especially 3 speed hub gears.

15

16

2 SPOKES

WHAT IS SPOKES??

SPOKES is a non-party voluntary organisation, founded in late 1977, with a membership by mid 1980 of 450. Our objectives and general philosophy are described in the inset.

ORGANISATION

SPOKES does not have a chairperson, a secretary, a president, or any conventional position except that of treasurer. Instead it is organised into a number of working groups (see below) which are set up as the need and the interest arises. Each group has its own co-ordinator. There is a general meeting every month at which a representative of each group reports back and where there is discussion of general campaigning issues. There is also an "interest meeting" each month at which we invite speakers or go out on "planning tours".

CYCLEPATH GROUP

The Cyclepath group is concerned with getting new cycleways built. They are running the long-standing Meadows campaign (see chapter 5).

The group is also looking at the possibility of a cyclepath/footpath from Roseburn and Davidson's Mains and Pilton (via the old railway lines) and then on to Queensferry and the Forth Road Bridge cycle track (via existing quiet back roads and paths). They are considering the possibility of constructing the railway section by voluntary labour and/or a Manpower Services project.

The group will also assist in campaigns for other routes, especially where there is a strong local demand.

EVENTS GROUP

The Events Group organises the annual SPOKES rally, complete with politicians, pipers, unicyclists, bicycle games, television and radio, and decorated bicycles. They also help other groups to run smaller events — like the Cyclepath group's Meadows rally in October 1979 and opening ceremonies for new cycle

facilities such as the Bread Street bus lane's opening to cyclists. The group is experienced in bicycle games (see Chapter 8) and co-operates with the Resources Group in organising games and displays at local community festivals.

Occasional socials are also held, and the donations of food from SPOKES members on these occasions are always especially noteworthy!

The group also run major campaigns of its own such as the 1980 "GO TO WORK ON A BIKE" campaign, in which 25,000 leaflets were distributed to motorists — nearly all in Lothian, but reaching as far south as the House of Commons!

NETWORK GROUP

The Network Group exists to inform cyclists of the most suitable EXISTING routes in Edinburgh and Lothian. Initial plans are for a series of 15 or so leaflets describing routes from the city centre to the suburbs: the leaflets to be sold in newsagents and bicycle shops as well as through SPOKES. Existing street maps of the city are often unsatisfactory because, being aimed mainly at motorists, they do not show "cut-throughs" and quiet back routes which may be ideal for cyclists and totally unsuitable for cars. See chapter 5.

A later stage of Network Group work will spread out into the Lothians.

PLANNING GROUP

The main function of the Planning Group is to keep tabs on local authority proposals which will affect cyclists, and try to ensure that the Councils live up to the policy on cycling in the Lothian Region Structure Plan. Some of the group's most notable successes include: the policy on provision for cyclists in the Lothian Region Structure Plan; Scotland's first contra-flow cycle lane (Lady Lawson Street; one of the first contra-flow bus lanes in the UK to allow cyclists (Bread Street); provision for cyclists in the McEwan Hall pedestrian precinct area; the Dumbiedykes cycle route; walkway/cycleways on disused railway lines in the Leith and Queensferry areas and elsewhere; and various road closures — through which cyclists are now allowed to pass.

In addition the group has taken a number of initiatives, putting forward plans for pavement widening, bus/cycle lanes and cycle parking on George IV Bridge, and organising a seminar of experts on provision for cyclists. The group also played a major part in the successful campaign for the cancellation of plans for fast new inner-city "approach roads" (see chapter 6 for a full account of Planning Group activities).

RESOURCES GROUP

The Resources Group has a variety of tasks, concerned with publicity, organisation and membership. It is the nearest thing SPOKES has to a secretary.

The group runs the SPOKESHOP (see below). Printed publicity leaflets are produced three times a year, and distributed by bike to around 1,000 different addresses throughout Lothian, including not only members, but councillors, officials, and related organisations.

The group also handles membership. and ensures that the talents, interests and skills of members are as widely used as possible. The membership forms ask people in what ways they can help (e.g. delivering leaflets, typing, helping at stalls etc.), and the Resources Group draws up lists of helpers which are then circulated to other groups.

SAFETY AND THEFT GROUPS

These are both relatively new groups. Both have already completed detailed surveys of SPOKES members — almost 200 replies were received. The results are described in chapters 3 and 4, and both groups are planning to use the information gathered in campaigns to increase safety and to reduce theft.

The Safety Group has also conducted an experimental "pothole reporting" experiment, and the Theft Group is conducting an investigation of bicycle insurance in conjunction with FREEWHEELING Magazine.

WHAT YOU CAN DO

We very much hope that you will decide to join SPOKES even if you don't have the time to help actively. In pressing our case with the authorities it is very important for us to be able to say we are speaking for a large membership.

If you have time, *you are invited to join a SPOKES working group and/or to attend general meetings.* Details of groups are given on our latest publicity leaflet, and you cand 'phone the group co-ordinator to find out the date of the next meeting. You are welcome to attend various groups to see which interests you best. Times of general meetings are also given on our latest leaflet — or 'phone SPOKES at 031-225 6906.

Even if you cannot help regularly, you may be able to help occasionally by manning a publicity stall, doing some typing, delivering some leaflets, or helping in other ways — see membership form.

Donations are always urgently needed to finance our campaigns and publicity. Cheques payable to SPOKES.

HOW TO JOIN

To join SPOKES all you have to is to write to SPOKES at 2 Ainslie Place, Edinburgh EH3 6AR (tel. 225-6906) enclosing a SAE. We will then send you a membership form.

WE LOOK FORWARD TO HEARING FROM YOU!!

SPOKESHOP

SPOKES sells a wide range of articles at stalls and by mail order. These include badges, stickers, envelope re-use labels, safety materials (reflective/fluorescent tape etc.), books, fact sheets, advice notes and submissions to the local councils.

The titles of our fact sheets to date are:

No. 1   Lothian Region councillors — wards, phone numbers, committees, cyclists
No. 2   Edinburgh District councillors — wards, phone numbers committees, cyclists
No. 3   How to write to an official
No. 4   Bike shops in Lothian
No. 5   What to do in an accident
No. 6   How to make a press release
No. 7   Interview from Network News: Stewart Parker talks about SPOKE-SONG
No. 8   Cycle Parking — including addresses of local suppliers
No. 9   Press and media addresses in Lothian and Edinburgh

For full details and pricelist please send SAE to SPOKESHOP, 2 Ainslie Place, Edinburgh EH3 6AR.

Councillor Brereton

SPOKES got off to a particularly auspicious start thanks to the outspoken views of Councillor Ralph Brereton, who was at that time chairman of the District Council Planning Committee, Councillor for Marchmont, "and proud of it". His letter to *The Scotsman* (5th May 1978), which is reprinted here, will remain an all-time gem in the annals of the city's transport history. *The Scotsman* was so deluged with outraged replies from cycling housewives, vicars, etc. that it only took ten days for the councillor to write again to *The Scotsman* to say that "a cycle track may be the answer".

The City of Edinburgh District Council.
May 3, 1978

Sir, — SPOKES can get lost. When all the pious rubbish has been said the reality is this: most cyclists in this city are students who live in Marchmont. And they want to ride through the Meadows on their way to the university. That's what is really going on. Never mind that the paths through the meadows are footpaths. Never mind the "no cycling" notices. Never mind the old people. Never mind the children. Never mind the mothers with shopping. Just let the hooligans blast through at 20 miles per hour and terrify the rest of us.

Never. Parks are for quiet, decent people. SPOKES can get lost and take its Commie friends with it. Who wants a proletarian dictatorship anyway? Not me, and not Marchmont.

Ralph Brereton,
Conservative Councillor for
Marchmont and proud of it.
The text of Councillor Brereton's letter to The Scotsman, 5th May 1978.

SPOKES OBJECTIVES

1. To encourage cycling and to publicise its benefits for the community and for individuals.
2. To ensure that council policies actively encourage cycling and make full provision for it, as part of an overall transport strategy through which all members of the public can enjoy cheap, safe and efficient travel for work and leisure.

Until recently the needs of motorists have been the overwhelming priority for public expenditure, with public transport coming a poor second, pedestrians even further down, and cyclists nowhere at all. SPOKES believes that the Council should have an overall transport strategy in which cyclists, pedestrians, public transport and private motor traffic are *all* taken fully into account, together with their effects on each other and their costs and benefits for the City and the Region.

This should imply, we believe, increased support for public transport, pedestrians and cyclists, and selective restraints on private motor traffic, particularly at peak periods. *It is within this framework that SPOKES campaigns for cyclists.*

HOW TO STOP YOUR BIKE GOING DOWNHILL.

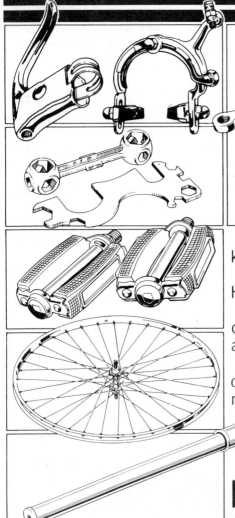

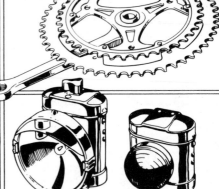

It doesn't take much effort to keep your bike properly maintained.

Particularly when you stop at Halfords.

Where you'll find a wide variety of good quality parts to fit bikes of all shapes and sizes.

From wheels, brake assemblies, chains and saddles, right down to nuts, bolts, cans of oil and puncture repair kits.

So don't come a cropper. Come to Halfords.

HALFORDS

Your local Halfords stores are at 138 Lothian Road and 14 Hanover Street, Edinburgh.

3 Safety

SPOKES BICYCLE ACCIDENT SURVEY
By SPOKES Safety Group

INTRODUCTION

The official statistics on bicycle accidents cover only those accidents which are reported to the police. Any accidents which do not result in hospital treatment or which are not reported to the police go unrecorded in accident statistics. In order to gain some idea of the nature of these recorded accidents, we conducted a postal survey of SPOKES members in early 1980, asking about accidents that they had had in 1979. A full copy of the report is available from SPOKES. Overall we found that 84 per cent of the accidents recorded in the survey had not been reported to the police.

Of the 170 respondents, 100 had had no accidents in 1979, 50 had had accidents which were not serious, and 20 had had accidents which involved either more than minor bruising or quite a bit of damage to the bicycle.

AGE AND SEX

A higher proportion of males than females had had accidents. This may be connected with distance cycled per week. Age did not seem to be an important factor — but note that our survey included very few children, and three-quarters of respondents were aged between 20 and 40.

DISTANCE CYCLED

Accidents seemed to occur more for cyclists who cycled over 20 miles per week, as might be expected, but the nature of the roads on which the cycling takes places is also important. Negotiating South Bridge, for example, appears more dangerous than cycling from Corstorphine to Haymarket.

TIMING AND SEASON

As would be expected, the majority of accidents took place between October and March although 37 per cent were in the summer months. There was a notable difference in the time of day when accidents were serious and when they were not. 40 per cent of the serious accidents occurred in the morning rush hour while only 14 per cent of accidents which were not serious occurred then. It did not appear that cycling after dark was unduly hazardous.

SAFETY DEVICES

One-third of those who had not had accidents wore bright or fluorescent clothes but almost half of those who had had serious accidents did wear such clothing! A higher proprotion of those who had had serious accidents used spacer flags than those who had not. It seems unlikely that the use of such aids increases one's chances of being involved in a serious accident, but we did not ask if the aids were being used when the accident occurred. It is possible that having an accident leads to an increased awareness of the need for conspicuity and other safety aids.

CAUSES OF ACCIDENTS

The most common individual reasons given for serious accidents were obstacles or holes in the road, and vehicles either pulling out of a side road or turning right (Table 1). Pedestrians were the major cause of less serious accidents. However, 60 per cent of serious accidents and about half of all accidents were related to motor vehicles. Respondents admitted that in about quarter of the accidents they were at least partly to blame for the accident.

TABLE I
CAUSES OF ACCIDENTS

Cause	% of serious	% of non-serious	% total
Pedestrian into road	11	21	18
Obstacle/holes in road	22	17	18
Vehicle out of side road	19	7	10
Car door opening	7	10	9
Vehicle turning right	15	6	8
Vehicle turning left	4	10	8
Vehicle moving off	7	7	7
Ice	4	9	7
Vehicle from behind	4	4	4
Animal	4	3	3
Vehicle while turning	4	1	2
Other	0	4	3
Number	27	71	98

INJURIES AND DAMAGE

In over half the accidents there was no injury to the cyclist, the majority of the remaining accidents involving only minor bruising or grazing. In only one of the 98 accidents was there a head injury. In 5 accidents the bicycle was a write-off and 24 accidents resulted in a bent wheel or forks. Over half of the accidents resulted in no damage to the bike. Virtually all accidents were harmless to other people, only 3 accidents involving minor bruising or shock to a pedestrian.

CONCLUSION

Although there are dangers in cycling, our sample of *adult* cyclists shows that cyclists are not themselves dangerous. Few of the accidents were 'self-inflicted', and a clear majority were caused by circumstances outwith the control of the cyclist. This being so, it is not surprising that such features as the age and sex of the cyclist are of little significance in discriminating between those likely to have an accident and those who do not have accidents. Distance cycled is a significant feature, but one has to take into account the character of the roads — especially since many accidents are caused by obstacles and holes in the road.

The dangers of cycling arise primarily from the manoeurvres of motor vehicles, but pedestrians and road conditions each caused nearly one-fifth of the accidents reported in the survey. Most accidents involved either no injury or only minor injury to the cyclist and *no significant injuries were caused by cyclists.* Most accidents resulted in nil or minimal damage to the bicycle involved, but 30 per cent

did have a bent wheel or worse. The answer to these real dangers is a combination of education of other road-users, pressure for high standards of road maintenance and appropriate facilities for cyclists, and sensible, defensive (but not deferential) cycling.

AN OFFICIAL PERSPECTIVE

Most accidents in our survey were not reported to the police and few caused any serious injury. What accidents are reported to the police?

In the first 16 weeks of 1980 the South Police Division of Edinburgh recorded 500 accidents not involving cyclists and 18 involving cyclists. Three of these involved no motor vehicle. The recording of accident details for the other 15 *implies* that in eleven cases (73%) the motorist was more at fault than the cyclist.

Cyclists involved in reported accidents are at much greater risk of injury and of serious injury than are motorists, though the sample of cycle accidents is small.

Of course, because many bike accidents are fairly harmless and are not reported these figures exaggerate the dangers of cycling.

The cyclist's age was recorded in 10 cases: 3 were under 10 years old; 3 were 18-20; 3 were 24-26 and one was in his 50s. This does not match the national peak of (reported) cycle accidents being in the 10-14 age group.

Official statistics underestimate the number of accidents which involve cyclists. They do record the serious accidents — especially those involving injury — but official statistics are open to different interpretations (see "The Bicycle Planning Book" by M. Hudson for further information).

	Accident involving cyclist (%)	No cyclist (%)
No injury	28	75
Slight injury	50	19
Serious injury	22	6
Total number	18	500

AVOIDING ACCIDENTS

Here are some guidelines towards safe cycling.

(1) Keep your bike well-maintained, paying particular attention to tyres, brakes, lights, reflectors and steering. Remember it is illegal to cycle without effective brakes, and at night without front and rear lights and a rear reflector, so carry spares on longer journeys.

(2) Wear white or light coloured clothes, especially at night; preferably with fluorescent strips or patches for day-time visibility, and white and/or reflective strips or patches at night. Spacer flags have been shown by the TRRL to increase the amount of room which motorists give to cyclists, though on the other hand they increase the amount of room which cyclists must allow to cars when 'traffic jamming'.

(3) Cycle deliberately (don't dither or wobble) and give clear hand-signals in good time.

(4) Always look behind when altering course, whether turning right or left, changing lanes, or just moving out to pass a parked vehicle. Then look behind again: remember motorists may ignore, or may not see your signals.

(5) Always know what is going on all around you. When stopping behind a motor vehicle it is best to position yourself where the driver can see you clearly in the mirror.

(6) Don't cycle in the gutter — keep two or three feet out from the kerb or from parked cars. This way you avoid the broken glass, wet leaves and other rubbish which accumulates there. It also gives you a distance to react when pedestrians suddenly step off the pavement: they expect to hear you.

(7) Be ready to alert others to your prescence with a loud bell/horn/bellow.

(8) Although slip-streaming buses might save you some energy it is extremely dangerous and in wet weather, plain suicidal if the bus suddenly stops. Remember buses have the right of way once they start to pull out from bus stops, don't start to overtake once the right indicator flashes on.

(9) When using roundabouts or turning right use the same lane as a car would. At large roundabouts such as Newbridge or Charlotte Square it maybe best, however, to keep in the left hand lane, and signal right at every exit you are not taking.

(10) Above all, anticipate the incompetence of others; car doors will suddenly open in front of you — assume any parked car with the driver inside will do this, and give it a wide berth (but remember to check behind before moving out). Cars overtaking you just before a junction may turn left in front of you. Be ready to stop.

The next section is intended to prepare you if unfortunately you do have an accident.

INSURANCE

It is advisable to be insured for Third party risks in case you cause injury to other people or property. This is very unlikely to happen, but the damages awarded against you may be very high indeed if it does. Third party insurance is usually included with policies for theft or damage to your bicycle (but check that it is), and also comes free with membership of some cycling organisations.

WHAT TO DO IF AN ACCIDENT HAPPENS

In some cases the cyclist will obviously not be fit to do much — but fortunately injuries are minor in most accidents.

An accident occurs very quickly, and it may take a few moments for you to realise exactly what happened — at best you are likely to feel shaken. Inevitably you will feel at a disadvantage relative to the motorist who will literally have taken it all sitting down. It is therefore very important to know in advance what you will do, as you may not be capable of working this out at the time.

Motorists' reactions to an accident vary enormously. At one extreme they may be very apologetic and worried that they have caused the slightest injury. At the other extreme they may be abusive, enraged by the scratches to their precious paintwork. Resist any natural temptation to lash out, either physically or verbally. Your position will be much stronger if you are polite but firm throughout. Keep calm, and:

(1) Note the **vehicle registration number** immediately, in case the vehicle makes off — this does happen sometimes.

(2) If there are no independent witnesses, **call the police immediately** from a nearby shop or house, having first informed the driver that you intend to do so.

(3) Get the **names and addresses of any witnesses**. This cannot be overstressed. Without a witness it is your word against the driver's, and you will find it more difficult to win a subsequent case in court. People may have disappeared by the time you have sorted things out with the driver, so ask someone to act as a witness before tackling the driver.

THIRD PARTY INSURANCE MEANS THAT

WHEN YOUR BRAKE CABLE SNAPS (60p) AND YOU SWERVE TO AVOID HITTING A DOG (PRICELESS)

AND SO CAUSE A CAR (£2500) TO SWERVE TO AVOID HITTING YOU INADVERTANTLY BUMPING INTO A LAMPPOST (£80)

WHICH CRASHES THROUGH THE WINDOW (£40) OF AN ART GALLERY AND GIVES THE CURATOR (£200000) A HEART ATTACK, DROPPING A MING VASE 30000 ON THE FLOOR

THEN ALL YOU PAY FOR IS THE BRAKE CABLE: THE INSURANCE COMPANY PAYS THE REST

INSURANCE

FOR SALE to pay debts

CLOSED UNTIL FURTHER NOTICE ●

Having a witness lined up before you approach the driver will also show him or her that you mean business.

(4) Get **the driver's name and address.** The driver is not required to give the name of his/her insurance company and may also be unwilling to for fear of losing the no-claims bonus — but try to get this nevertheless.

(5) Note any damage to you, your bicycle, and other vehicles.

(6) Draw a map showing the location (with measurements if possible!), any traffic signs or controls, and what you were both doing. Note the time and the weather. This can all be very useful in court, if things go that far. A photograph of the street can also help.

(7) **DO NOT** admit blame or say you were sorry, even if at the time you think it was your fault. If you admit blame, you may jeopardise your insurance claim.

(8) **Report the accident to the police** IT IS VERY IMPORTANT TO DO THIS, EVEN IF THERE IS NO INJURY:

If the driver is convicted of drunken, dangerous or careless driving, or some other offence, it will improve your chances of getting compensation. You should press for charges in all such cases.

The Highways Department decide where to install safety features partly by the number and type of accidents for which a full police accident report is made, so ask them to make a full report. The more such reports are made, the greater the number of safety features intended to help cyclists which will be installed, and the stronger the case for special cycle facilities.

Any accident causing personal injury (however minor) and involving a motor vehicle MUST be reported by law.

WORTH REMEMBERING

It is an offence to open or cause or permit to be opened any door of a motor vehicle so as to cause injury or danger to any person. This means that a driver could be convicted even if one of his doors causes a cyclist to swerve only.

It is an offce to leave a vehicle on a road in such a position or in such circumstances as is likely to cause danger to other persons using the road. It is therefore a good idea to note the numbers of any parked vehicles which may have contributed to an accident, even if they are not directly involved.

Remember the golden rules:
GET THE CAR NUMBER
GET A WITNESS
GET THE POLICE if necessary
DON'T ADMIT ANYTHING and
DON'T GIVE UP EASILY.

POTHOLES

Any cyclist in Edinburgh will soon discover problems of negotiating defective road surfaces. Despite legislation placing responsibility on the local authority to ensure that roads be maintained in a proper condition, potholes and other rough road surfaces appear faster than the Highways Department is able to maintain them.

Any cyclist who rides disregarding rough surfaces will soon either have buckled wheels or at best wheels knocked out of true. Defective road surfaces are also a cause of accidents. To avoid potholes often requires evasive action and swinging wide into the traffic stream is an obvious hazard.

SPOKES Safety Group encourages all cyclists to make strenuous efforts to encourage the repair of rough road surfaces. We suggest the following guidelines:

(1) Telephone or write to the relevant sub-regional engineer of the Highways Department. The addresses are as follows:

Edinburgh — D. McLean, 4 Rothesay Terrace, Edinburgh. Tel: 225 7144.

East Lothian — K. Minty, Alderston House, St. Martins Gate, Haddington. Tel: 062-082 4131.

Midlothian — J. Bruce, Kippielaw, Lauder Road, Dalkeith. Tel: 663 9595.

West Lothian — I. Johnston, Thornton House, Falkirk Road, Linlithgow. Tel: 329 2191.

General Letters and Complaints should go to the boss, Mr. A.. Crocket, Director of Highways, Lothian Region, 19 Market Street, EH1 1BL. Tel: 229 9292 Ext. 2401. SPOKES may design a special "pothole postcard", but in the meantime you can get one from the Secretary of the Cycling Council of Great Britain, 69 Meadrow, Godalming, Surrey.

(2) **It is essential to describe the exact location of the pothole** i.e. Street, outside house no ..., side of road, distance from kerb, nature, along with your name and address for acknowledgement.

(3) Several complaints from different individuals are likely to be more effective than single complaints.

(4) Initially choose the worst, biggest, deepest potholes. Those on busy roads are most likely to be attended to.

(5) If you get angry at the state of the roads in general write to your local authority, councillors and your MP.

CLAIMING DAMAGES

If your bike is damaged by a particularly bad pothole, write to The Director of Administration, Mr. A. McNicholl, Lothian Regional Council, George IV Bridge, Edinburgh EH1 1UQ, describing the damage to your bike, (and to you) naming the exact location of the pothole and stating your intention to send them later a receipt for any necessary repairs.

REFERENCES

The Penguin Book of the Bicycle (Watson & Gray: 1978) has a section on safety which is illustrated with examples of common traffic hazards (pp 299-306).

Richard's Bicycle Book has a very good chapter (6) on urban riding or 'traffic jamming', which should be read by every cyclist at least once a year.

'On your bike'. A guide to cycling in London (L.C.C. & F.C.E. : 1979) has a good chapter on cycling safely (pp 5-7).

The Bicycle Planning Book by Mike Hudson (1978) is useful especially Chapter 3.

The information on what to do in an accident was taken from SPOKESFACTS No. 5 (1979): "Accidents: what to do if you have one".

All these books are available from SPOKES

Further Reading

FREEWHEELING magazine frequently has articles on safety. See Safety First 'The need for training' (July 1979, pp 18-19); 'Accident' (Dec. 1979, pp 15-15); and 'The Work of the Transport and Road Research Laboratory' Jan. 1980, pp 14-15).

Finally the SPOKES Safety Group is always glad to help and advise cyclists or prospective cyclists.

FRIDAY FOR BRIAN AND ME

I felt the tension mounting inside and I gulped down the last few mouthfuls of toast and marmalade, snapped on my clips and rolled down the garden path into the avenue.

This was friday: a special day of the week. Not just because it's the last working day but every Friday Brian and I race each other to work. Brian lives just around the corner; the corner where we met at 8.15 precisely, the usual time. Brian was dressed in his customary charcoal suit with fluorescent yellow clips. I had on my light grey suit with blue glitter clips.

Brian nodded and we raced off into the wind, skidding round the numerous corners of the local side streets before streaking out along the main road into town.

Horns blared, women and children scattered as we raced, two abreast, down the High Street, both of us familiar with this opening move and knowing that the real battle was to come.

A double-decker pulled out in front of us. We separated and rode one each side of the bus. As Brian passed the cab, he tossed in a firework. We met at the front and slowed down to a snails pace before moving off around the next bend.

As I travelled passed a queue waiting for the bus, my hat was knocked off by an outstretched arm. Brian turned his head as he saw this and laughed. So doing, he didn't see the car door opening in front of him. The door was sheered off as Brian hurtled through.

Suddenly Brian was pulling away from me but I sped on, passing a Jag here, and a Lotus there, as they ground to a halt in the morning rush hour. I could see Brian at the next set of lights so I put my feet down and accelerated rapidly. My spacer flag bent backwards due to the air pressure, and the diamond tip scrapped the side of a bus as I whipped through a narrow passage in the traffic to emerge into a wide free space and zoomed round a roundabout cutting across three lanes of motorists.

I flew on, and then as I moved over to cut across the oncoming traffic and made a right-hand turn I noticed an artic, bearing down at a ferocious speed. I had to move fast. I dived to the ground and as I lay quite flat together with my bike, the lorry drove over, its wheels either side of us. It screeched to a halt 50 yards further on, but by that time I was out of sight, catching Brian up with every second.

Traffic was building up at the next set of lights. I filtered through between lanes and hit the junction as the lights changed. I was over before their fingers started moving to release the hand brakes.

Not hearing my approach a man stepped out into the road. I swerved behind him, lifted off his bowler and put it on my head to replace the one I had lost. I was very near Brian now but he made the next set of lights before they turned to red. I screeched to a halt, leaped off, ran over the junction and remounted on the other side. I knew then that I'd catch him. As Brian tried to weave through several lanes of traffic at the next junction, I moved into the clear oncoming lane, overtook 200 metres of vehicles and met Brian at the front.

We grinned at each other as I caught up and we pretended there was some fault with our bikes whilst the lights were at green. The horns blasting behind us and we moved off on amber leaving them standing there as we weaved round each other along a perfectly clear road. This was the last stretch into Ferranti Ltd. where I work as an accountant and Brian as area sales manager.

By Bill Clarke of CYCLEBAG

4 Theft

'Where's My Bike?'

CYCLE THEFT

Cycle theft is the bane, or at any rate a bane, of the cyclists's life. Having parked your bike and spent a distracted half hour away from it (distracted by wondering if you'll ever see it again) it's bittersweet to find both bike and padlock still there on your return. If only someone would steal the padlock — a great iron thing — and leave the bike!

Time endears you to your machine. You grow accustomed to its pace. In return for your love, it moulds its saddle to comfort you. You buy parts for it. It stands by you in times of need. You love it, and it loves you! It's a hard blow when you come back suddenly to find only an empty space and a violated padlock. There's an empty space in your heart that takes a long time to heal.

This may sound exaggerated — but only if you've never had a bike stolen. For the next day or two, you don't believe it. You ask all your friends if they've borrowed it. You keep looking where you left it, expecting it to have been there all the time. You look in the most unlikely places. Then you begin staring at cyclists in the street, suspecting each one to be on your bike. You report it to the Police. It's like reporting a death. You report it to your insurance company. They send a death certificate to fill in. Your practical life is messed up because you have no bike and you have to walk, bus or taxi. It costs time and money. And when eventually you obtain a replacement, it isn't a replacement at all. It's a new machine, a new personality, a new relationship. It can't replace the old one any more than one person can replace another.

Sadder, and wiser, you allow your life to build again. The pain eases. And then an article like this stirs it all up again.

SPOKES CYCLE THEFT SURVEY

INTRODUCTION

The SPOKES Theft Group began meeting in early 1980. There was no doubt that cycle theft was a problem that was already severe and getting worse. Police statistics recorded over 2000 thefts a year in Lothian. This works out at an astounding rate of one theft every 4 hours 20 minutes, day and night.

The group began its fight against theft with a survey of SPOKES members. The aim of the survey was to collect some systematic information about the extent to which SPOKES members had suffered from cycle theft, and the circumstances in which the thefts took place. SPOKES was becoming increasingly concerned at the number of reports of cycle thefts from members and other cyclists in Edinburgh, and it was hoped that a survey of members would help to set priorities for any future campaign to improve the situation.

The survey was carried out by means of a short questionnaire sent to all members with the 1980 membership renewal forms. Members were asked to complete the questionnaire and return it to SPOKES. The questionnaire asked for the following information:

(1) The usual type of lock used (if any) and the method of locking used.
(2) Details of thefts of whole bikes, including how recently the theft occurred, where the

bike was stolen from, the method of locking used at the time of theft and the type of lock used, if any. The questionnaire had space for up to two bike thefts to be recorded.

(3) Information on the impact of the theft on the cyclist: whether the theft was reported to the Police, whether the bike was recovered, whether it was insured and if so, what percentage of the replacement value was obtained from the insurance company.

(4) Information on thefts of pumps, lamps, wheels and so on.

CONCLUSIONS

These are the conclusions we have drawn from the returned questionnaires. Our conclusions have to be tentative. Between 75% and 80% of members rejoining SPOKES in 1980 returning the questionnaire. So the tables which summarise these returns are completely accurate as a description of the respondents, and are a reasonable guide to all SPOKES members. We are not sure how they relate to all cyclists. (We know, for example, that SPOKES members are almost all adults, while many cyclists are young people. So the survey can only be a guide to thefts from adult cyclists).

% of thefts by method of locking in use at the time of theft. (% of respondents using that method normally in brackets)

to itself	42%	[9%]
1 wheel to fixed object	7%	[12%]
frame to fixed object	13%	[31%]
wheel and frame to fixed object	20%	[47%]
not locked	18%	[1%]

1 Total Thefts
37% of respondents have had a bike stolen. Even taking only thefts in the last year, one respondent in three had a bike stolen. We think this is alarmingly high.

2 Sex
Males are more likely than females to have a bike stolen. 50% of all male respondents suffered theft compared to 29% of females. We have no idea why.

3 Age
The age group most at risk is 20-29 years. But note that most SPOKES members are in this range, so this survey may be missing a lot of theft of young people's bikes.

4 Theft is not the Cyclist's Fault
Bike thefts are not usually the result of negligence on the part of cyclists. 82% of bikes stolen were locked at the time, either to fixed objects or to themselves.

5 Method of Locking
Lock your bike to a fixed object! (It's comforting when your own SPOKES survey produces common sense). 91% of respondents who have never lost a bike normally lock them

to fixed objects, while only 40% of all stolen bikes were so locked at the time of theft. Also, people who have never lost a bike always lock it. Almost all lock it to a fixed object. Unfortunately, it doesn't follow that if you copy these people, you won't lose your bike.

6 Type of Lock
No Lock is completely secure, but some are overcome more often than others. 42% of respondents who have never lost a bike use a heavy chain and padlock, while only 23% of all stolen bikes were secured in this way. On the other hand, 'other' locks — mostly the combination type — seem rather vulnerable. The heavy chain type is foiled much less often than the 'other' types. The wire types lie in between. The same story is told even if you consider only those bikes locked to fixed objects.

7 Police Statistics
92% of the respondents' bike thefts were reported to the Police. This could mean that the Police statistics are pretty accurate and that there is not an enormous number of unreported thefts. Or it could mean that people who report bike thefts are the sort of people who join SPOKES and return questionnaires.

8 Recovery
About one bike in five was recovered.

9 Place of Theft
Most bikes are stolen from home. Presumably bikes spend a lot of time at home too, so it doesn't follow that homes are any more risky than other places. But one thing does follow — bikes are not necessarily safe at home. Home here means, inside or outside a home or tenement stair. The remaining thefts were from the office or place of work or from outside shops and places of entertainment.

10 Insurance
About half of the stolen bikes were insured. 42% of the resulting claims were met with a payment of full replacement value. However, due to the wording of the question, it is not clear whether 'replacement value' means the insured cost of the bike, or the cost of getting back on the road again. Nonetheless, given the high theft rate and the low recovery rate, it seems sensible to insure your bike.

11 Minor Thefts
Most minor thefts are of lamps or pumps, and nearly everyone had suffered this. A few people (12% of respondents) had lost other items, saddle bags and panniers being the most common targets.

Thefts by type of lock in use at time of theft (% using that type normally)

heavy chain and padlock	23%	[47%]
long thin wire	21%	[23%]
short thin wire	32%	[21%]
other	24%	[9%]

LOCKS

Security and convenience are the keywords here. The most secure is the **thick U-bolt type lock.** However, as well as being very difficult to cut or break it is inflexible and will not easily secure your bike to certain available fixed objects. It can also be heavy and expensive.

Not so secure but more convenient is the **padlock and chain.** Both should be of case hardened steel and the chain should be encased in moulded plastic (or a length of old inner tube) to prevent scratches to your bike. The longer the chain the greater the number of objects you can secure your bike to, though the more weight you have to carry with you. A **padlock and length of wire** can be relatively inexpensive and light. The wire must be of an adequate strength, though, and is easier to cut than a chain.

Virtually all locks can be picked but especially so the cheaper ones made of softer metal. **Combination locks** do not appear to be any more successful than padlocks.

Most thieves are opportunists, though, and everything you can do to delay them a few more seconds will greatly increase the chances of their being detected or discouraged from stealing **your** bike.

A 'Sheffield' bike rack at a location in Sheffield.

CYCLE PARKING

Where and how you park your bike can have a considerable effect on the potential cycle thief. Bikes are most secure when they are parked where they can be clearly seen by passers by, security guards, servitors etc. Similarly, bikes are most secure when the parking place allows the frame to be locked to whatever the bike is being parked against or in.

These are simple rules but unfortunately they are too often forgotten by those concerned with providing parking facilities at offices, factories, places of entertainment etc. The most common reaction is simply to ignore the needs of cyclists altogether.

This is not important if there are plenty of substitutes in the form of railings, parking meters or even drain pipes. Fortunately, the centre of Edinburgh provides extensive railings for parking the bike whilst shopping or nipping into the pub and the SPOKES cycle theft survey found that only 19% of thefts occurred while parked at this type of location.

The real problem is to ensure that employers recognise the need for adequate parking facilities at places of work, (the New St. Andrews House fiasco (see next article) provides an example of how not to do it).

Parking Facilities

In addition to facilities for cycle parking at places of work there is also a need for some provision at public libraries, recreational facilities such as the Botanics and the Commonwealth Pool and shopping centres where railings are not available or inconvenient for the cyclist or passers by. A survey of cyclists preferences for cycle parking in public areas carried out by SPOKES early in 1979 suggested that the St. James Centre, George IV Bridge, Woolworths/Princes Street, the Mound, George Street and Chambers Street were the most preferred locations. Unfortunately, the Highways Department who are still trying to give effect to the Council decision of 1978 to install cycle parking in the city centre intend to concentrate their provision only at Chambers Street, George Street, the Mound and the Grassmarket.

A lot of the cycle parking facilities available allow only the front wheel to be held and locked. These are cheap and nasty and frankly not worth having. The concrete front wheel holders, (found for example, at the east entrance to the Botanics or Newington Library) are the worst of all and are notorious for bending front wheels.

What is the ideal type of cycle parking facility? SPOKES has brought out a factsheet which discusses all the important design features and comes down heavily in favour of 'the Sheffield Rack'. The fact sheet also lists names and addresses of local suppliers. If your office, school, swimming pool, library, factory or sale office is without adequate cycle parking, write for a copy of our factsheet (5p + SAE). Don't give your boss or union representative any peace until the racks are installed.

PARKING AT WORK — THE CASE OF THE SCOTTISH OFFICE

People who cycle to work often face the problem of what to do with their bikes when they get there. The problem is made worse because other people face exactly the same problem. Typically, the result is bikes in people's offices, bikes leaning against buildings, bikes clustered round trees and poles, while nearby a large open space is given over to car parking.

At New St. Andrews House in the St. James Centre, present site of the Scottish Office, cyclists were much better off. There are plenty of railings, and as we all know, railings are ideal for parking. These railings have the added advantage of surveillance by Security Guards at the entrance to the building, and they cost nothing to use as a cycle park.

Cycling has been endorsed by the Government on grounds of health, energy-conservation, and reduced congestion. It should therefore be entirely appropriate for the Scottish Office to encourage cycling amongst its own employees. But, regardless of this, they decided to ban the use of the railings by cyclists. The reasons were that bicycles are unsightly, that they blocked a fire exit and that they were liable to break windows. Perhaps the Minister for the Arts should be asked to determine whether bicycles are more unsightly than the ubiquitous car park! As for the possibility of breaking windows, this would be rather difficult as the windows are shatter-proofed against bombs! The fire exit is close to only a small part of the railings, and this reason cannot warrant banning the use of the whole railings. Cycling employees were not consulted before the change and they naturally protested.

By way of compensation, the Scottish Office provided a bicycle cage under the entrance to the St. James Centre, outwith the Security Guards' field of vision and that of passers-by. It was a steel frame covered with plastic coated wire mesh, with a lockable door. Every cyclist in any Scottish Office building was entitled to a key. Inside, there were concrete "wheel-bender" slots. It took months to build, and cost several thousand pounds. Cyclists protested that both the design and the location of the cage were an open invitation to thieves.

Within days thieves broke in, by cutting a few mesh links in the door to reach the handle inside. The Scottish Office had steel plates welded to the door. Thieves this time snipped the mesh at the side of the door, walked in, and were hidden by the steel plates while they worked on the bicycles inside. Thieves broke in again and again. We understand that New St. Andrews House now has the unenviable distinction of being one of the 3 worst places in Edinburgh for bicycle thefts.

It is clear that the cage was a costly mistake and will never be secure: it is out of sight and keys are widely available. The infamous cage was even featured in the Guardian, The Times and The Scotsman, but the motorised management remains obstinate. Cycling employees had responded by pointing out that as there were 'lavish parking facilities' for staff with cars it was only right that cyclists should have adequate facilities. They suggested that some of the visitors car parking area be given over to 'Sheffield' racks, pointing out that 10 bicycles could be parked in the space for one car by this method. The racks are comparatively cheap and would be under surveillence from security guards.

Subsequently the management decided to buy some Sheffield racks — but for use in the cage, not the car park. However, the racks have now been lying in the cage for months without being erected — the official reason for this being a lack of funds! Perhaps in years to come a new generation of management will have the sense to put them to use in the car park. Or perhaps they won't have the chance — we hear that an enterprising thief now has made off with one of the Sheffield racks!

The frustrating thing about the whole episode is that it was entirely avoidable. Not only are good cycle rack designs available, and not only could the Scottish Office have listened to informed comment on cycle parking provision, but there was not even any real need for change in the first place.

RECOVERY SCHEMES

This article is about methods of getting your bike back once it has been stolen or lost. There are several methods in use today; most notably the Police Force and the Cyclebag (the Bristol cycle group) Postcode scheme. These are discussed below. The idea of a National Bicycle Register is also described. No such scheme exists at the moment, though it has been suggested from time to time. I should say right at the start that SPOKES currently has no plans to introduce any recovery scheme, though we may do in the future. But first, let me clarify the terms used.

"Losing" a bike means having it stolen from you.

"Finding" a bike means discovering someone else's, apparently abandoned, and handing it in to some recovery agent like the Police.

"Recovering" a bike means getting your bike back after losing it.

Recovery is a touchy topic. It is based thoroughly on the idea of Private Property, which makes some people uncomfortable. The trouble with Private Property and owning things is the sneaky feeling that All Property Is Theft, but as this article is about recovery rather than about sneaky feelings, I won't take these points any further. *(Editor's note: nor will we!)*

33

Police Recovery

The main method of recovery today is the Police Lost Property Department. Most cyclists report their loss to the Police, who note details such as frame number, colour, model, size and so on. And if the bike is found, it is almost always handed in to the Police rather than any other recovery agent. However, not many stolen bikes are recovered this way.

One reason is that owners often cannot describe their bikes with any accuracy, especially the frame number.

Another reason is that there is no central record of stolen bikes. The Police Force is divided into regions, so unless your bike is reported missing and then found in the same region, it doesn't have much chance of being recognised.

A last reason is that bike theft is only one crime among many that the Police have to deal with, and it doesn't have a very high priority. An article in Police Review (13 June 1980) explains why it should have a higher priority. But even so we can't expect bike theft ever to become the number one crime.

The Cyclebag Postcode Scheme

Police recovery is not satisfactory. This is shown by the low recovery rate and by the large number of local recovery schemes that have been set up from time to time in different parts of the country.

One such scheme is the Cyclebag Postcode Scheme. What they do is stamp your Postcode and house number onto your bike frame. Cyclebag has the tools to do this and charges a few pence for it. If the bicycle moves to another address (or you move house, or sell it) then they just stamp an X against the old code and stamp the new code below it. So all the previous owners of a bike can be traced to verify the present ownership, and the present owner can be contacted if the bicycle is found. We haven't yet got around to asking Cyclebag how well the scheme operates in practice. On paper, the scheme suffers two main drawbacks.

As before, there is the problem of locality. If the bike is stolen and moved out of Bristol, and then found, do the Police know to look for a postcode? And if they do, have they the will and the resources to do anything about it?

Another problem is that it can take considerable effort to verify ownership. The crafty thief can stamp postcodes just as easily as Cyclebag can. So the thief can easily stamp her own postcode, or several of her own codes, onto the bike. Chasing up all the stamped owners, who may have left Bristol, to find the one owner who really owns the bike, is time consuming and expensive, and is, therefore, less likely to be carried out.

These are only paper objections, and it may be that the scheme works well in practice. You can find out from Cyclebag at 35 King Street, Bristol, BS1 4D2.

Registration Schemes

Registration schemes work by stamping a registration number on the frame, and entering the owner's name and address against that number in a book. When the bike is found, the owner can be traced. The idea of a bike register is anything but novel. Wherever you go it seems that either the local bobby kept a register in his spare time twenty years ago, or knew someone else who did.

But these schemes all suffered one problem in common; they were local. If a bike was moved out of the registration area, the register couldn't help to get it back.

Also, registration is a touchy topic. Some people agree strongly with the idea. To others the idea of a central register of bike owners seems to go against the idea of cycling as an expression of "small is beautiful", personal liberty, and feels like another step towards 1984. To some extent these objections can be sidestepped by making any registration scheme voluntary.

A National Bicycle Register

This doesn't exist, so don't panic. This is a description of how one could work, the advantages it would bring, and the problems it might have to face. We follow a bike through its life: from frame maker to dealer, then to the first owner, then the second owner, then stolen, recovered, and eventually scrapped.

First, the frame maker stamps a unique number on the frame. At the moment they don't do this. They stamp batch numbers. Also, there's no co-operation to ensure that two different frame makers don't use the same numbers. Under NBR, each maker has her own series of numbers to use. (In fact, the Dutch and German Police are asking the International Standards Board to do something on these lines already). The frame numbers correspond with records on the NBR central computer file held in, say, Edinburgh. NBR supplies the makers with a certificate, rather like a car logbook, for each bike. When the maker sends the bike to a dealer, she tears the certificate in two parts. One part goes to the NBR to say that the bike has been sold, and the other part goes to the dealer.

When the bike is sold, the new owner now has a bike and part of a certificate. If she doesn't want to register her bike with NBR (it's voluntary after all) she can just forget about the paper. In that case, NBR doesn't know anything about her. But let's assume she does register! She writes her name and address on the certificate and sends it to the NBR. She probably does this in the cycle shop when she buys the bike. There is a registration fee to pay.

When the NBR receives her form, it matches with a bike that was sent to a dealer and is not on the stolen list, so that's OK. NBR register her name and address and send her a new certificate, just like the one the frame maker had, with two parts. Thereafter, the owner pays an annual subscription to the NBR, keeps them informed of changes in her address and so on.

The years fly past and she decides to sell the bike secondhand. When she does, she gives the new owner one part of the certificate, and sends the other part to the NBR to take her name off that bike.

The new owner also registers. But alas his bike gets stolen. Quickly, he notifies NBR of the theft. The NBR periodically produces a list of stolen bike numbers — say once a week — on a medium such as microfilm. Copies of this list are sent all over the country to registered dealers in secondhand bikes, to public libraries, to main Police stations, to Customs Posts and to anyone who has a good reason for wanting one. Perhaps a reward is offered. Sooner or later the bike is found.

When the bike is found, the finder notifies NBR. NBR passes on the news to the registered owner, who arranges to collect his bike. In this way NBR can guarantee not to let out anyone's name and address to anyone else.

Eventually the bike is scrapped. The last owner notifies NBR, who take the owner's name off the list, and stop asking for the annual subscription.

Besides the advantage of effective recovery, you might expect insurance companies to offer a lower premium for registered bikes. But I believe there would be a much more dramatic effect: the market for stolen bikes would be destroyed. A thief could perhaps sell a stolen bike without a certificate, or even with a forged certificate, but when the new owner tried to register it the theft would become apparent and the thief might be caught. A thief could change the registration number, but a new number would either clash with an existing one or demonstrably belong to no bike at all. Bike theft for profit would disappear virtually overnight. So the main problem that the NBR would face is that it would put itself out of business!

But how about not losing your bike in the first place.

By SPOKES Theft Group

35

ODE ON A DISTANT PROSPECT
OF THE OLD COLLEGE
Nicolson Street, Edinburgh, 9.05 am

I hate the happy cyclist who
Goes whizzing past me in my car
As I sit in a traffic queue
Resentful, and not getting far.
I sound my horn self-righteously
As he goes by, as free as air.
Why he should pass, I cannot see.
I feel it simply is not fair.

For after all, he has not paid
A road fund tax, as once I did:
His transport has not, like mine, made
Him poorer by six thousand quid.
And does he care what I am spending
On petrol every single week?
And does he know the cost of mending
My latest radiator leak?

There is no point if (as is right
For me that is a Senior Clerk)
The firm should give me, marked in white,
A personal numbered place to park,
If, just to use the space at all
I have to leave in dawn's grey mists
And travel townwards at a crawl
Just to be passed by cyclists!

Ah! Do not think I have not tried
To re-assert the motorist's rights.
I use bus lanes, I pass inside,
I shout abuse, I flash my lights.
I make the cyclists scrape the kerb
As I squeeze through in front of 'em
To stop (positioning superb!)
To cause disruption maximum.
I open doors, in stratagem,
In front of cyclists passing by
Or sometimes just run into them
(Crude though it is). I really try.

And yet sometimes I wish that I
Were free as they are, gliding by
So silently, pollution-free,
So gently healthier than me —
But that, I see, is heresy
And fit but for an anarchist
Or mincing poove with dropping wrist ...
Not for a natural man like me
Of the twentieth century ...
Oh how I hate the cyclist!

5 Urban Routes

CAMPAIGN FOR A MEADOWS CYCLEWAY
By Alison Spears of SPOKES Cyclepath Group.

Why build a cycleway?

The Meadows is situated one mile south of central Edinburgh. Just to the north is the University, the Royal Infirmary, the Southside, and the Royal Mile; whilst southwards lies an extensive residential area. During the morning and evening rush hours, heavy traffic uses the roads and junctions east and west of the Meadows making cycling to and from work for those living to the south a hazardous occupation. Middle Meadow Walk is a wide thoroughfare which crosses the Meadows from south to north with ample room for both pedestrians and cyclists. It is well surfaced and it is a surprise to the newcomer to see "No Cycling" signs at either end, for it is surely a natural route for the cyclist.

The Campaign

The campaign began early in 1978 when SPOKES set up a Meadows Group. A first success was the discovery that the "No Cycling" signs were misleading. Edinburgh by-laws say that children under 12 years old can cycle on footpaths and there is nothing to stop them cycling in the Meadows. When the District Council was informed of this oversight, nothing happened. But when we offered to erect suitable signs ourselves the Council swung dramatically into action, so that the signs now read: "No cycling except for children under 12 years". Persuading the Council to change the rules for adults too has proved harder, but the campaign is now on the brink of success.

The Meadows Group prepared a well argued booklet called "The Case for the Meadows Cycleway". This proposed an extensive network (see map) which included routes especially built for cyclists; segregated routes on existing paths; shared bike/pedestrian paths and bicycle traffic lights at access points.

One of the signs in the Meadows.

Pedestrians' Rights

The plans also paid full attention to pedestrian rights. No cycle route was proposed along Jawbone Walk because of the high pedestrian flows and the existence of the cherry trees which prevented widening the path. Improved crossing facilities for pedestrians were proposed at the foot of Marchmont Road, and it was suggested that Tarvit Street be closed to all motor traffic except residential and deliveries.

There would be other benefits for pedestrians. Increased usage of the Meadows, especially at night, will be a deterrent to the occasional muggers etc. found in the area. Secondly, the existence of an official designated cyclepath should bring to an end the present irregular situation where a pedestrian can be surprised by a cyclist coming up behind and overtaking on Middle Meadow Walk. Finally, the Middle Meadow Walk cycleway will be a tremendous first, not just for Edinburgh, but for Scotland. It must be remembered that there is much experience of such facilities in other towns and cities in England and Europe. This has conclusively shown that pedestrians and cyclists can mix very happily where a scheme is well thought out. A survey on the cycle/pedestrian paths in Hyde Park in London showed that 90% of pedestrians said they were not inconvenienced. In Peterborough, cycle/pedestrian ways have been welcomed by both, and have cut the number of bike accidents in the city.

The next stage

The Meadows Group Proposals were presented to the District and Regional Councils along with a petition signed by several hundred local residents. Local people and groups were informed of the plans at public meetings where discussion was introduced by means of a colour-slide 'roadshow'. The District Council took no action on the proposals, but the Region felt that they fitted with their transport philosophy of improving public transport, encouraging more people to walk and cycle, and decreasing the use of cars in the city centre (with all their attendant problems of congestion, noise, pollution, etc.)

David Bellos (original co-ordinator of Meadows campaign) with Councillors Cairns and Gorrie (far right).

It soon transpired that the Regional Council was able to be more than just interested. For Middle Meadow Walk had been passed to the Highways Committee of the then Edinburgh Corporation in the 1950s, so that it could be maintained and lit by the Highways Department rather than by the Parks Department. Thus responsibility for Middle Meadow Walk remained with the Highways Department of the Lothian Regional Council when local government reorganisation came in 1974. Of course, the Park itself is the responsibility of the Recreation Committee of the City of Edinburgh District Council. This unusual allocation of responsibilities meant that the Transportation Committee of the Regional Council could ask their officials to draw up plans for a cycle way on Middle Meadow Walk, provided that it did not stray onto the Park itself.

The Regional Council's Plan

Thus in 1979 officials of the Highways Committee drew up plans which involved setting aside a strip of Middle Meadow Walk with priority for cyclists. The plan also included the erection of appropriate signs and the installation of traffic lights at Melville Drive and Teviot Place to allow cyclists safe access to the road system at either end. New traffic lights require approval from the Scottish Development Department and so the scheme was submitted to them by the Region. This caused a very considerable delay, because the SDD decided to ask questions about the powers under which the Regional Council intended to designate a cycle path on Middle Meadow Walk, and because SDD themselves were novices (and apparently not enthusiastic either) when it came to facilities for cyclists.

During this period the SPOKES Meadows Group became the Cyclepath Group, with a wider brief to campaign for cycle routes on disused railway lines and (where appropriate) in other parks. Constant lobbying was essential. Whenever we dragged our feet we found that a letter from the Region to the SDD (or vice versa) had lain untouched in an in-tray for months. Through our leaflets we encouraged individual members to write to relevant MPs and Councillors. A high point of pressure was our October 1979 Meadows Convergence Rally when, despite atrocious weather, hundreds of cyclists from all parts of the city converged on the Meadows and symbolically pushed their bikes down Bruntsfield Links and up Middle Meadow Walk. We were led by the newly elected Councillor for Holyrood/Meadows ward, Willy Roe, who is now a member of SPOKES and of the Regional Transportation Committee. The local MP, Robin Cook, was also roped in on more than one occasion, and by those means progress was kept up, albeit at a grindingly slow pace.

In Spring 1980 the Scottish Development Department agreed to authorise the traffic light scheme on an experimental basis.

The District Council's Objections

At about this time it became apparent that some District Council officials were not pleased about the proposals and so had raised more legal problems. Who, they said would be liable if a child were injured by a bike on the cycleway and under what powers was the Region going to build that cyclway? The lawyers of both Councils were consulted and a legal opinion was sought from Senior Counsel to determine the solution to this knotty problem! It transpired firstly that reponsibility, in the unlikely eventuality of such an accident, would be the same as if a child ran into a road, and, secondly, that the Region does indeed have powers to build a cycleway in Middle Meadow Walk. However, Counsel also advised Lothian Region to seek the agreement of the appropriate committee of the District Council before going ahead and that is what is happening right now as we write in the autumn of 1980.

Finally

Let us all hope that the District Council agrees with the proposals so that the benefits for all concerned which we listed above will be at last realised. The Middle Meadow Walk Cycleway, of course, is an experiment. If it succeeds, as we believe it will, then we look forward to a more fruitful co-operation in the future between District, Region and central government to ensure comprehensive networks of cycleroutes not just for north-south and east-west crossings of the Meadows, but wherever conditions justify them in the City and in the Region.

SPOKESWAYS
TOWARDS A NETWORK OF CYCLE ROUTES
By Ken Moore of SPOKES Network Group

If you cycle in Edinburgh, or in any other city, you must have noticed that there are problems. There is, for example and above all, the motor traffic. Noisy and dangerous, it crowds you, cuts in front of you, terrorises you, and makes you choke on its fumes and in the end, if you are particularly unlucky, maims you or kills you. There are other special problems, appreciated only by cyclists who, almost alone, use the part of the road closest to the kerb. There, the broken glass, rusting metal and other debris are strewn like rice at a wedding. It is there that the pedestrians who look on the first yard of the road as an optional extension to the pavement step suddenly in front of you as you come downhill on a wet day with wet brakes. It is on that part of the road that the drain covers, bars spaced at the width of a bike wheel, wait to throw you off. Because as a cyclist you usually have to keep well to the left, you are forced time and again to swerve out into the traffic by illegally parked cars, cars that swoop in to park in front of you, cars that are waiting to leave side streets while sticking halfway out into the main road. The potholes and the undulating (or simply broken-up) road surfaces, and the rocking manhole covers, are everywhere; but somehow especially at the sides of the road, no doubt because there they inconvenience cars least and so are last to be put right.

To these features of all towns, Edinburgh adds its own specialities. Because of its situation, it offers lots of steep hills and is often able to provide a stiff adverse wind. Because of its age, it is well furnished with cobbles, whose effect on a bike is enhanced by frequent lifting and incompetent re-laying. And it has a good supply of one-way systems, traffic lights and islands, roundabouts, prohibited turns and assorted arbitrary restrictions designed with the private motorist in mind, or just occasionally the pedestrian, but never (until SPOKES) the cyclist.

It is a bleak enough picture. Various national surveys (for example one conducted under the auspices of the Road Transport Research Laboratory) have confirmed that it is problems of this sort — especially the ones to do with motor traffic — which people most often say put them off cycling. To be fair, it must be pointed out that this is what people SAY. There is also some evidence that even if such obstacles to cycling are removed as can be removed, people still won't cycle if apparently soft options for the individual, such as taking the car to a guaranteed parking space at work, are available. The fact that these soft options are bad in the long run for the individual's health, and through the damage they cause to the environment to other people's health as well, does not always weigh too heavily with the average lazy and selfish human being. Still, the balance of probabilities is surely that more people would cycle if the problems could be lessened; and certainly those who are cycling already would enjoy it more, or be encouraged to keep it up, if that could be done.

Networks of Cycleroutes

So what can be done? Ultimately, of course, and in the ideal world, there should be a system of cyclepaths serving all parts of the town. They would connect with the rest of the road system at convenient and safely designed junctions, and would link housing, shops, workplaces, places of entertainment. Their surfaces would be smooth and well-maintained, innocent of any hazards put there by the public utilities and kept free of the hazards put there by bottle-breaking, can-discarding vandals. All the gradients would be gentle. Where the pedestrians shared the cyclepath, they would show some respect for their own skins, and yours, as you do for theirs. There would be ample cycle parking, offering support and security against theft, wherever it was needed. And, to make it perfect, it would never rain or snow, and every wind would be behind you ...

But the ideal world is still some way off, and meanwhile we must make the best of what we have in Edinburgh, such as it is. Until these problems are *eliminated* by a rational transport policy, could they not be *avoided* meantime by a cyclist choosing the best routes? Yes, to some extent (is the answer), but it's tricky. Existing street maps of Edinburgh or of anywhere else so far as one knows, are just about the worst way of deciding how to cycle from A to B if you don't know the terrain between A and B. They are designed (you guessed it) for motorists. They don't show cut-throughs, places where you can easily wheel your bike for two minutes for a saving of ten minutes, streets where none but the confident or well-insured cyclist would go. (Some of them don't even show on-way streets, which must inconvenience motorists too.) And, of course, they don't show steep hills, cobbles, bad surfaces or good places to park a bike.

The obvious solution would be to produce a map of Edinburgh which is designed for cyclists — a splendid longterm project! Meanwhile, SPOKES Network Group decided on a different approach. Instead of trying to guide the cyclist through every path on to which he/she might stray, the task would be tackled from the other end. In the first place, likely journeys for cyclists (in the jargon called travel desire lines) would be identified. Secondly, the best route for these journeys would be ascertained by actually cycling over the alternatives. Finally, the results of these researches would be published in a series of pamphlets:

THE SPOKESWAYS

Identifying the likely journeys was relatively easy because Edinburgh has a very radial road system. So it was the work of a month or so (helped by the publications of Lothian Region) to define nineteen radial routes, from the centre to the outskirts, and seven peripheral ones, not passing through the centre, but by the districts which, roughly, they had to serve.

THE "BEST" ROUTE

But deciding what is the "best route" for a journey is less easy. Ask ten cyclists what is the best route between here and there, and you will get twenty different answers (Cyclists are twice as good as mere individuals). Some kind of order and method has to be imposed on his creative chaos, and the Network Group came up with an Order of Priorities (if you're a cyclist, I bet you don't agree with it.) Best routes should be:

1. **Safe**
2. **Legal**
3. **Easy on the rider**
4. **Easy on the bike**
5. **Pleasant**

First, the route should be safe. This means that your chances of being mauled by a macho motorist should be as low as possible, and that means that, wherever possible, a Spokesway should go by side streets instead of the main road. But, as usual in a complicated world, there are exceptions. On the one hand, Edinburgh does have bus lanes on some of the main roads, and cyclists are allowed to cycle in them (although some bus drivers don't seem to have entered into the spirit of the thing). The consequence is that, if you really must cycle on a main road, it is often better to do so on one that has a bus lane than on one that doesn't, especially during the rush hours when the bus lanes are officially operative. And the curious thing is that drivers tend markedly to keep out of bus lanes even outside the operative hours: so on some roads, the bus lanes are best even at midnight. Local knowledge is needed. But on the other hand (you will have to glance back to see where the first hand was!) side streets which are palpable ways of avoiding the traffic jams are likely to have been spotted by motorists too. It may not be such a wizard wheeze after all to cycle along a pitted side street which is being used as a rat-run by commuting motorists. Since they have been smart enough to perceive the short cut, they may be exceptionally impatient of the mere cyclist who prevents them from exceeding the speed limit on this very narrow and twisting back street. Local knowledge is needed.

But there is more to safety than merely avoiding heavy traffic. Roundabouts, devised by the motorist for the motorist, far from perishing from the earth, grow in Edinburgh apace, even at the minimum junction of three roads. As a general rule, you should venture on them only if you are prepared to give way, not only on entering, but at every exit to drivers cutting in front of you, and in between to drivers who would have liked to have made a career as stunt men. As a rule, right turns are safer with traffic lights. Local knowledge is needed.

In Edinburgh, the legality of where you may cycle is governed by an obscure mixture of national and local Acts. It is quite likely, for example, that you may legally cycle along a stretch evidently intended for pedestrians only, if it is not parallel to a highway, unless there is a clear prohibition on cycling (are you following me?) displayed at either end or there is a general legislative instrument to the same effect. To be legitimate, you should possibly wheel (or perhaps carry) your bike over the stretch in question. Nevertheless, legality comes after safety in our list. The choice must be yours, and SPOKES most certainly does not advise you to break the law. Legality is an equally obscure matter for the motorist — see "The Uncontrolled Crime Wave" (Chapter 7).

Then we come to the less ticklish subject of routes which are *easy on the rider.* Edinburgh is a hilly city and we must acknowledge that not all cyclists are as superbly physically fit as the present writer. If your journey involves a hill which cannot be avoided, need it all be done at once? Is it possible, by a series of sallies into side streets, to break the thing up so that although travelling further on the map, the cyclist actually takes less time to win the summit? Then again, no-one who has gone up the same hill with cobbles and without cobbles, so to speak, would have any hesitation in telling which is preferable. And, while on the subject of cobbles, they are best avoided on the level too, unless you are an exercise freak with a taste for vibro-massage. As for going downhill on cobbles, there is no more hair-raising, teeth-rattling experience: trust to the fit of your wig and your dentures. Cobbles, in short, for all their prettiness and artistic integrity with Georgian or Victorian Edinburgh, are a sair fecht for the cyclist. By the way, they are slippery when wet, which is much of the time.

Next, there is the question of finding routes which are *easy on the bike.* This is related to the previous question of routes which are easy on the rider, and, as with it, a lot can depend on the bike: but here the order of advantages is reversed. A hill which is not too bad on a lightweight racer with good low gears, for example, can be beyond the limits of human performance on a solid heavy tank of a bike with one fixed gear. But when it comes to rough going, the heavy job tends to stand up to it rather better. Still, there are some general principles which will hold for all types of bike, which brings us back to cobbles again, especially cobbles downhill. They are an excellent way of

loosening all the nuts and bolts on your bike, some to the point where bits start to drop off to be crushed by the closely following traffic. It really cannot be recommended. Potholes and other types of bad and damaged road surface tend not to be fixed features, not because they are quickly repaired, but because new ones keep appearing, sometimes literally overnight. Nevertheless, some have become such semi-permanent features that it is prudent in drawing up recommended routes to warn against them.

Finally, if after all this there is still a choice, Spokesways are chosen to be as pleasant as possible: scenic, architecturally interesting, not passing the glue factory. Such routes do exist in Edinburgh, sometimes surprisingly close to busy and polluted thoroughfares. And it must be remembered that cycling is, after all, enjoyable; and it can be enjoyable even in a city, even now.

Pamphlets describing the SPOKESWAYS will soon be on sale for a very modest sum, considering the experience that is crammed into them.

NO LEGAL EXCUSE FOR INACTION

By a Lawyer

Local authority officials often excuse their failure to create cycleways by blaming the law for not giving them clear powers to do so, but it is really a very poor excuse.

Edinburgh District Council can use section 50 (1) (a) of the Edinburgh Corporation Order Confirmation Act 1967 to lay out any part of any park for cycling and could, if they wanted, create miles of cycleway within months. The carriageway across Bruntsfield Links, or the Cramond promenade are obvious candidates which could cater safely for walkers and cyclists with no more alteration than the painting of a white line. The safeness of this type of provision has been proved in Stevenage and Hyde Park, London, (see 'The Bicycle Planning Book').

The prime responsibility for the provision of cycleways, however, lies with the highway authority which is the Secretary of State for trunk roads and the regional council for others. Section 3 (1) of the Trunk Roads Act 1946 gives the Secretary of State power to construct cycle tracks alongside any trunk road whether it is already in existence or is being newly built. The CTC opposed this type of provision in the thirties fearing that cyclists would be banned from the road itself, but are motor vehicles banned from ordinary roads because they now have motorways reserved for their exclusive use? In city streets the regional council could use its power under Section 1 (1) (c) of the Road Traffic Regulation Act 1967 to provide cycle-only lanes and could thereby create even more miles of cycleways in a very short time at very low cost.

Nor is there any legal difficulty in creating cycleways which strike out on their own across town or country. Regional councils have powers to acquire land compulsorily or by agreement for the creation of highways and may add to their list of highways any private street or linear route. They can then make an order under the Road Traffic Regulation Act restricting the types of vehicles which are allowed to use the new highway. A local example where this was done to the detriment of cycling is the Western Approach Road where only certain classes of motor vehicles are permitted. The order could have had exactly the opposite effect with all motor vehicles prohibited had the regional council so desired!

I knew everyone in SPOKES was mad. I heard they even have a Psychopath Group.

How can bikes move without pedalling? — Is it cyclekinesis?

Q: Why is cycling down The Mound like making it in show business?
A: You've got to have the brakes.

Say NO to National Bicycle Week

Issued on behalf of the Friends of Urban Motor Transport League and Anti Self-Righteous Cyclists

RID OUR ROADS OF THE TWO WHEELED MENACE

British democracy and fair-play demand that as the pedalling fanatics creak and gasp their way through the overcrowded streets and headlines, the people must have the right to decide on the available evidence whether or not the bicycling cranks and environment-alists are to be encouraged. This leaflet, which outlines the case against bikes, is shortly to be distributed to every household by vans and pedestrians.

PEOPLE WHO RIDE BICYCLES

o CAN CAUSE APPALLING POLLUTION
o THREATEN MASSIVE UNEMPLOYMENT
o WILL UPSET OUR FOOD AND OIL DEMANDS
o ENDANGER BRITISH SOVEREIGNTY
o PUT FURTHER STRAIN ON THE HEALTH SERVICE
o GET IN THE WAY OF CARS AND MANY PETS

One of the 'juggernaut' bikes which could become a common sight on British roads if cyclists are allowed to get their way.

CYCLISTS AND WORLD ENERGY RESOURCES

At a time of global world food shortages and increased prices, cyclists make profligate waste of this essential commodity, demanding almost three times the intake of an average motorist in barley water and Mars bars alone. Just one week's continual cycling is enough to reduce most people to the point where they are obliged to eat far more than is healthy in order to make clothes fit. Oil supplies, too, are badly hit. The shortfall in demand normally put aside for motoring cannot be met by the manufacturers of puncture outfits, handlebar flasks or luminous saddlebags.

CYCLISTS AND POLLUTION

Tests have shown that during periods of prolonged warm weather or in hilly areas a mass of perspiring cyclists can cause hazardous changes in the climate, blotting out the sun with a wall of acrid steam and exhaled gases which can be fatal to small roadside rodents and wreak havoc on a hedgerow. Bicycles, which are not subject to MOT testing, litter the highways with spent spokes, mudguard stays, thermo-plastic reflectors, dynamo parts and sections of oily chain. None of this detritus is bio-degradable.

CYCLISTS AND BRITISH SOVEREIGNTY

In recent history, no democratic nation has survived the indignity of its head of state being obliged to pedal to important state occasions. There is no evidence that H.M. The Queen is a competent cyclist, or that she would be prepared to wear pumps in the interests of state security. Military experts have pointed out that troop movements by bike could badly impair Britain's strike capability in the event of war.

CYCLISTS AND THE HEALTH SERVICE

Hard-pressed doctors cannot be expected to cope with a rush of cases caused by a sudden epidemic of cycling. Among the hundreds of ailments cyclists risk, the most dangerous are chronic haemorrhoids, seized and arthritic joints, exposure, carbon monoxide poisoning and giddy spells on stiff climbs.

CYCLISTS AND OTHER ROAD-USERS

Cyclists accidentally run over to impaled on passing cars can cause severe and costly damage to bodywork, trim and suspension of even the most sturdily-built motors. They aggravate the already fatiguing stresses on the motorist by forcing him to decelerate or change course. Cats, hedgehogs, mice, badgers and voles which do not usually impair the progress of vehicular traffic can upend cyclists, clogging busy junctions and spoiling the look of the countryside. Pedestrians, too, are at risk from the noise of bicycles. Because bicycles make no noise, you can easily miss them and get knocked down.

Bicycles are increasingly polluting the urban environment warns a leading scientist.

CYCLISTS AND YOUR JOB

Cyclists make no secret of their determined campaign further to threaten unemployment in the motor industry and allied trades. In general, cyclists jeopardise productivity by arriving for work often late, wet through, or in no fit state to rebuild a better Britain.

KEEP BRITAIN FREE OF BICYCLES

Reprinted by kind permission of PUNCH

Over population of cyclists could destroy valuable habitats warns an environmentalist.

6 Planning for the Cyclist in Edinburgh

By SPOKES Planning Group

INTRODUCTION

Cycling is already an important form of transport in the Edinburgh area, particularly as a means of commuting to work : cyclists are in evidence on all the major routes and many of the back streets, and any large office or institution has its fair share of cycles parked nearby. Unfortunately, this simple message and the more important point about the *potential* of cycling as a mode of transport has simply not yet registered with many of the officials in the Highways Department and elsewhere who are obsessed with the needs of the motor car. Despite continued lobbying by SPOKES for some 3 years and increasing recognition at the political level — the needs of cyclists are still largely ignored. Traffic schemes are implemented with undesirable effects for cyclists and little effort is put into positive planning for cyclists. There is the clear impression that cycling is seen as an emphemeral fad, the occasion for a quick snigger before getting down to the serious stuff of planning the next road, monster roundabout or maze of one-way streets.

This chapter looks at various aspects of planning to meet the needs of cyclists in Edinburgh. It contains information on cycle use in Edinburgh derived from various surveys carried out by SPOKES members and a demonstration of how the designs and plans of the Highway engineers commonly have adverse consequences for cyclists, how you can find out about these plans and, if necessary, fight back. Finally, the chapter explains what positive planning for cyclists in Edinburgh might involve and gives examples of some of the ideas that SPOKES has floated.

CYCLE USE IN EDINBURGH

The Lothian Region Discussion Paper "Transportation in the Edinburgh Area" (June 1979) declares that: "compared with the total volumes of traffic, the number of cyclists is insignificant". To check these claims and to test our suspicions that official traffic counts tend to undercount cyclists, SPOKES has carried out a number of cycle surveys during the past two years, concentrating on the peak 8 am to 10 am periods. The results of these surveys are shown, along with the date at which the information was collected, in Table 1.

TABLE 1 : NUMBERS OF CYCLISTS COUNTED AT VARIOUS JUNCTIONS
8.00 AM to 10.00 AM

	SURVEY DATE			
JUNCTION	10.5.78	27.6.79	8.5.80	(14.2.79)
Tollcross	238	243	247	154
Melville Drive/ Buccleuch Street *	199	152	200	123
South Clerk Street/ Hope Park Terrace	150	100	134	
Haymarket	x	153	162	
Queensferry Street	x	139	128	
Morningside Station	x	x	133	
Foot of Leith Walk	x	x	29	
Abbeyhill †	x	x	55	

* 8.00 AM TO 9.45 AM ONLY
† 8.00 AM TO 9.30 AM ONLY
x Junctions not included in the survey at that particular date

TABLE 2 : BICYCLES IN COMPARISON WITH TOTAL TRAFFIC
8.00 AM to 10.00 AM

Road	Bicycles	All vehicles	Bicycles as a percentage of all vehicles
Haymarket Terrace	77	3570	2.2
Queensferry Street	98	3230	3.0
GPO — Princes Street	42	1890	2.2
GPO — North Bridge	62	2326	2.6
Causwayside (Dick Vet)	176	2125	8.3
South Clerk Street	96	2267	4.2
Bread Street	40	1552	2.6

NOTES: Cycle figures taken from SPOKES surveys; total traffic figures taken from the June 1979 Discussion Paper, Technical Appendices Figures T/12 and T/11 using the percentage breakdown of traffic during different times of the day provided in Figure T/2.

The figures suggest that bicycles form an important part of peak period traffic at several junctions. Table 2 shows the results of the cycle counts at various streets in Edinburgh given as a proportion of the total traffic figures for the same roads taken from the Appendices to the Lothian Region Discussion Paper. Although such estimates are bound to be approximate, they suggest that bicycles already account for between 2—8% of all traffic at the peak period. Since the same report estimates that heavy goods vehicle traffic in the city centre was only 4.4%, should we regard heavy vehicle traffic as "insignificant"? Of course not, but neither can cycling be written off as a marginal activity.

But all counts of traffic at major roads and junctions ignore the cyclists who choose safer back routes. To date SPOKES has not undertaken a comprehensive survey of possible back routes, but a survey carried out in connection with the campaign for a contra-flow

Frank Howie

An early SPOKES survey.

cycle lane in the southern half of Lady Lawson Street on 27th February 1980 examined the use of the West Port area by cyclists. Apart from showing a flow of 66 bikes from 8 am to 10 am the directions taken suggested that many cyclists were by-passing major junctions such as Tollcross and, possibly, Haymarket. This points to the need for further detailed surveys at sites near major junctions. Abbeyhill, for example, may be by-passed by a fairly quiet journey via Royal Park Terrace and Spring Gardens; if the aim is to travel to and from the University or South Side.

SPOKES, however, would be the first to accept that the actual number of cyclists — using major thoroughfares or back streets — is considerably less than the potential. Almost all adults can cycle and a large proportion own or have the use of a bike. Too often, potential cyclists are deterred by fears for their safety on busy roads designed for motor traffic. To realise this potential, transport planning has to recognise the needs of cyclists through:

Full consideration for cyclists in all road, traffic management, and other traffic planning schemes.

A series of special measures for cyclists (often linked with new measures to assist pedestrians).

ROAD, TRAFFIC MANAGEMENT, AND OTHER PLANNING SCHEMES

In this section we give examples of how cyclists' journeys are made longer, more dangerous, and more daunting, and how opportunities to benefit cyclists are missed, in many new road, traffic management, and planning schemes. At the time of writing (July 1980) there had not been *one* single such scheme brought forward by the Highways department on their own initiative in which there was the slightest evidence that cyclists had been considered from the outset — and there had been many examples where this could easily have been done at relatively minimal cost.

"Traffic management" schemes

Traffic management schemes are measures to alter the flow of traffic on existing streets by means of special lanes, one-way streets, traffic signals, signs, etc. They can be used to benefit cars, buses, pedestrians or cyclists, or any combination. In practice most such schemes seem to be designed primarily to speed the flow of motor vehicles. Pedestrians often lose as much as they gain: extended stretches of railings lengthen journeys, traffic lights at junctions make it necessary to wait twice to cross diagonally, and traffic is faster and so more noisy and dangerous. As far as cyclists are concerned, journeys are often lengthened, no special measures are included, and in some schemes the result is that large numbers of cyclists have little choice but to undertake either dangerous or illegal manoeuvres.

The *Tollcross traffic management* scheme is an example of what can happen when this type of proposal is implemented. It would take considerable space to describe all the problems that have been created for cyclists but 3 examples will illustrate the position:

(a) The one-way system in Lady Lawson Street (southern end) and Lauriston Street force cyclists travelling from Haymarket to Lauriston Place either to make a detour through the dangerous Tollcross junction, or to make an illegal U turn from Bread Street to Lauriston Street, or to get off and push their bikes along Lady Lawson Street.

Map A

PEDESTRIAN ISLAND & SIGN — PREVENTING U TURNS FROM BREAD ST.

BREAD STREET   WEST PORT   LADY LAWSON ST

LAURISTON ST

ONE WAY & COBBLES

LAURISTON PLACE

Thanks to a SPOKES campaign, Lady Lawson Street is to get an experimental contra-flow cycle lane.

(b) The complex 5 way junction was created at Tollcross forcing cyclists to have to turn across fast moving traffic in several cases.

(c) The one-way street system in the Glengyle Terrace, Valleyfield Street, Tarvit Street area forces cyclists travelling from Gilmore Place or Bruntsfield Place to

49

Lauriston Place or Melville Drive to travel through Tollcross or to dismount or cycle illegally. SPOKES has suggested that Tarvit Street be closed to through traffic by bollards at one end and access allowed for cyclists in both directions. Eventually this could link into a cycle route alongside North Meadow Walk.

Map B

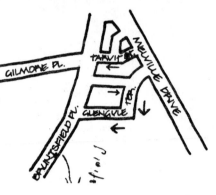

SPOKES HAS SUGGESTED THAT TARVIT ST. BE CLOSED TO THROUGH TRAFFIC BY MEANS OF BOLLARDS AT ONE END & ACCESS ALLOWED FOR CYCLISTS IN BOTH DIRECTIONS.

Roundabouts

Roundabouts are probably the most dangerous and difficult features of the road system for the cyclist, with fast-moving motor traffic often cutting in front. More complaints have been received from SPOKES members about roundabouts (especially Crewe Toll and Leith Walk) than any other aspect of road design. A cynic might suppose that the continual introduction of new roundabouts (sometimes removing traffic lights at the same time) by the Highways Department was another measure designed specially to keep cyclists' numbers down. New roundabouts in the pipeline include: Fountainbridge/Gardeners Crescent, Milton Road/Leith Approach Road, Cameron Toll, Lady Road/Dalkeith Road. No thought has been given to cyclists in any of these schemes — although in the most potentially dangerous — the Milton Road roundabout — there is to be an extensive system of pavements and subways for pedestrians, which could have been designed for use by cyclists also.

Map C

LEITH WALK ROUNDABOUT.

- - - → CYCLIST
═══⟩ MOTOR VEHICLE

High speed stretches of road

Although there have been no urban motorways built in central Edinburgh (unless one counts the Western Approach Road), there have, nevertheless, been several cases of short stretches of road "improved" to high speed standards. Leith Street, Earl Grey Street and the new £1 million Potterrow whizz-way encourage cars to go fast, and cause difficulties and danger for cyclists who have to cross the road. At Potterrow pedestrians have at least been catered for by a subway (only one mugging so far), but despite the high level of cycle use in the area, the Highways department has totally ignored cyclists. Although the University has agreed to allow cyclists to use the McEwan Hall precinct, and Highways officials were aware of this decision from mid-1978, no access between the precinct and the road system at the North end has yet been provided. Predictably, many cyclists now faced with the choice of an illegal maneouvre or a long and dangerous detour, choose the former.

50

Map D

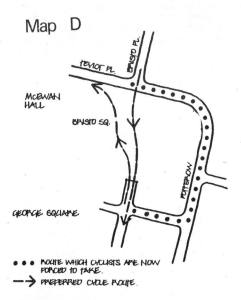

● ● ● ROUTE WHICH CYCLISTS ARE NOW FORCED TO TAKE.

→ PREFERRED CYCLE ROUTE.

Road closures

Road closures which block streets to traffic in some way can be of various sorts including:

(a) the pedestrianisation of a former street;
(b) the blocking of one entrance to a road to traffic;
(c) the stopping up of a road for some new development, for example, for a new road or a new use for the land.

In many cases, particularly (a) and (b), SPOKES supports road closures — indeed they are an essential means of controlling misuse by cars — providing adequate account is taken of the needs of cyclists. Too often cyclists are simply banned along with all other traffic, or obstructions are created which force cyclists to dismount. SPOKES has even been told that it is illegal for cyclists to push or carry their bikes through the Rose Street pedestrian precinct. Worst of all, insensitive road closures can deny cyclists access to quiet back routes, and force them onto busy roads. A particularly blatant example was the proposed closure of South Gyle Road/Cultins Road, to the south west of Corstorphine. SPOKES, the CTC and individual members of SPOKES objected to this closure, which would have cut off the only local quiet route to the lanes of West Lothian, and have forced recreational cyclists to use either the busy A71 (Calder Road) or the quite horrific A8 (Glasgow Road). At the time of writing, it now looks as if the local authority will inplement a scheme to allow continued access for cyclists, following these objections.

Commuting by car

Lothian Region is committed to discouraging commuting into the city centre of Edinburgh by car. But in practice too little is done to implement this policy by the officials and the stream of cars (often containing only one person) into Edinburgh clogs up the major road arteries, slows down buses and other essential traffic and acts as a deterrent to many potential cyclists who are not prepared to brave the fumes, the noise, and the danger. This connivance at car commuting takes many forms. Charges for long stay parking have been ludicrously low at many of the gap site car parks and only now are there plans to increase them. It is also found in the lax enforcement of car parking controls in streets and the reluctance to extend the controls to areas which are well within walking distance of major central offices. Stricter control over the creation of parking spaces at new office developments is also required — the present standards applied by Edinburgh District are far too lax.

Planning Applications for New Developments

Developers have to advertise their proposals for public objections. Cyclists seem never to be considered explicitly by the developers or, sadly, by the planners whose job it is to evaluate these proposals. The two main deficiencies relate to cycle parking and safe access for cyclists. The most blatant recent example is the massive Cameron Toll shopping/office/recreational development. This £20 million scheme will include 1000 car parking spaces, and its associated road system will create serious problems for cyclists by replacing two traffic light junctions by roundabouts. No consideration has been given to cycle access or parking even following detailed official objections by SPOKES. The same is true of all planning proposals at present: for new housing schemes, office blocks, or whatever.

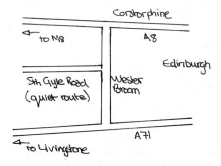

51

HOW TO FIGHT BACK

It is essential that cyclists actively campaign both to prevent the creeping deterioration described above and to promote positive alternatives. This is easier said than done — the experience of SPOKES, over the past 3 years, is of continued official indifference so that disproportionate effort is required to achieve quite minor improvements. Nevertheless, SPOKES has found that consistent and painstaking campaigns can pay dividends and the more that cyclists press for recognition in this way, the more they will succeed in establishing themselves on the political agenda.

To help individual cyclists and those who are active members of community groups to join the campaign for better recognition of the needs of cyclists, we have prepared the following guide. There are 3 basic principles:

Make sure you know what is being proposed for your area or for any part of the town in which you cycle regularly — this is far from easy but we have tried to set out the various sources of information below.

Make sure the officials preparing the plans are aware of your views and if you do not like what is being proposed — object. Again we have set out the existing procedures for objections and how the relevant bodies have to deal with them.

Make sure that you involve your local councillor and local community group. This will add weight to your campaign and although some officials are sympathetic to cyclists, it is prudent to assume they are not. It is essential to communicate directly with relevant councillors to ensure that they are aware of your case and do not have to reply exclusively on their officials' interpretation of your point of view.

The transport planning maze — how to find your way about

There are a range of documents and procedures which collectively shape the conditions the individual cyclist meets on the road. These vary from broad policy statements (for example, Transport Policies and Programmes and Structure Plans) to more specific sets of proposals (for example, Local Plans and traffic management schemes) which in theory, at least, are intended to implement the policy statements. The guide to this maze set out below is far from comprehensive but we hope that it will give you sufficient information to launch a campaign on a specific issue.

1. Transport Policies and Programmes (TPP'S)

TPP's (Transport Policies and Programmes) are periodic statements of transport policies and their likely financial consequences over the next 5 years. Until recently these were prepared annually but the Government has just announced that this is to change to every 4 years, with annual up dates. TPP's are the most important statement of policy on transport matters, but, surprise, surprise, there is no obligation for the local authority (the Region in this case) to seek comments or views or even to publicise their contents. SPOKES has found it exceptionally difficult to get hold of a copy of the TPP until it has been approved by the Region — when, of course, it is too late to influence what is decided — despite the Region's commitment to "open government". However, the controversy over transport policy in Edinburgh and, in particular, the conflict between the urban road programme contained in the first 3 TPP's (the system started following local government re-organisation in 1975) and the declared policy commitment of the Region to favour public transport, produced a period of public consultation in 1979 following the publication of the Green Paper on Transport Policy (new roads to you and me) and a public exhibition. The proposed urban road system was decisively rejected by the public and, subsequently, by Lothian Region but elements of the plan have still survived in the current TPP — particularly the expensive proposals for new city centre car parks. Again bicycles hardly rate a mention. For copies of the current TPP write to the Director of Highways, 19 Market Street, Edinburgh and try your councillor if this does not work.

2. Development Plans

Under the Town and Country Planning (Scotland) Act 1972 the main basis upon which planning applications are decided, and the building proposals of local councils spelt out, is the statutory Development Plan. It has the advantage over the TPP that by law the public have to be consulted for their views and ideas during its preparation, and if they are still not satisfied can formally 'object' to the Secretary of State. The Development Plan is however limited because it can only deal with land use and development. It is composed of 2 complementary parts:

(a) Structure Plans

These are documents which lay out the Regional Council's broad policies (i.e. attitudes and intentions) for those things which affect the whole region, or a large part of it. Hence they can sound a bit vague, but these policies add up to the kind of future which the Council wish to bring about in the region, and collectively they form the plan's strategy (i.e. its overall direction). SPOKES used the legal right to be consulted during the preparation of the Lothian Structure Plan to get a broad policy on cycling written in to the plan. This says: "the Regional Council will co-operate with the District Councils to implement schemes that will allow greater freedom of movement to pedestrians and cyclists and encourage more people to walk and to cycle for work and leisure journeys".

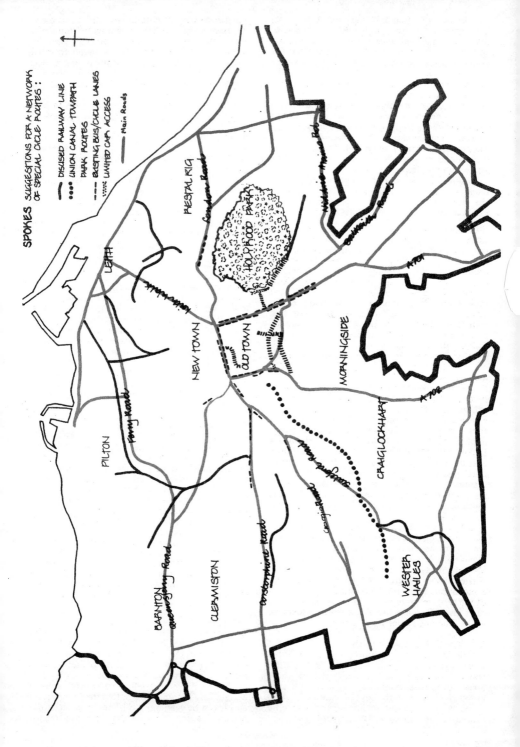

SPOKES SUGGESTIONS FOR A NETWORK OF SPECIAL CYCLE ROUTES :

DISUSED RAILWAY LINE
UNION CANAL TOWPATH
PARK ROUTES
EXISTING BUS/CYCLE LANES
LIMITED CAR ACCESS
Main Roads

RESTALRIG

HOLYROOD PARK

Cordiner Road

Arthur's Seat Park

Craigmillar Road

LEITH

NEW TOWN

OLD TOWN

MORNINGSIDE

A701

A702

PILTON

Ferry Roads

CRAIGLOCKHART

Craiglockhart

BARNTON

Queensferry Road

CLERMISTON

Corstorphine Road

WESTER HAILES

In general, Regional authorities in Scotland have a statutory obligation to publicise the survey material on which the plan is based and the draft plan itself, to allow time for public representations, and to hold a type of inquiry, called an Examination in Public, into matters which the Secretary of State considers require public examination at which the various points of view are publicly debated. Following the Examination a report by the chairman of the inquiry, the Reporter, goes to the Secretary of State. The Secretary of State ultimately has the power to modify the plan before approving it. Subsequent alterations to the Structure Plan also require his approval.

One of the main functions of structure plans is to provide a framework for preparing the second part of the development plan, local plans.

(b) Local Plans
Local plans will eventually take the policies of the structure plan and enlarge upon them to the point where they mean something on the ground. In Edinburgh they are being prepared by the District Council for areas like Leith or Currie-Balerno. As well as a written document they therefore contain maps showing which pieces of land are affected. Again there is a statutory obligation to publicise a preliminary statement, called a discussion paper in Edinburgh, to seek views, and to hold an inquiry if there are any subsequent objections to the draft plan (called at "written statement"). Although the idea of a Local Plan for a distinct neighbourhood sounds nice, in practice the planners are often dependent on others to get their proposals implemented. For cycling and transport in general this means that the District Council's plans have to be implemented by the Lothian Region Highways Department. Nevertheless, SPOKES has found that the Local Plan machinery offers a means of putting specific ideas for improvement into the system and in some cases, for example, walkways and cycleways on disused rail lines in the Leith area, there have been some very real benefits.

Copies of Discussion Papers for each Local Plan (and the survey material on which they are based) are obtainable from the Director of Planning, Edinburgh District Council, 18 Market Street, Edinburgh. When a new Discussion Paper is produced it is usually given some publicity in the "Evening News". Copies of the Written Statement and proposals map for each Local Plan are also available for inspection at the Planning Department office.

3. Traffic Management Schemes
Traffic Management measures are implemented under the Road Traffic Regulations Act 1967 and this provides the framework within which local authorities publicise and advertise proposals and deal with any objections. Before drawing up an order to implement a specific proposal, the Highways Department is usually obliged to consult with organisations representing road users — SPOKES is now on the list of such organisations. This gives advance warning. Later on, if the proposals are taken forward, the order will be published in the public notices column of the "Scotsman" and/or "Evening News" and notices tied to lamp posts etc. in the area concerned. These give details of how to object and who to object to. However, to confuse matters, orders are often made initially on an "experimental" basis and objections only sought when the "experiment" is made permanent — this can be some considerable time after the changes have been made on the ground. In most cases, any objections will simply be considered by the Transportation Committee, which means that it is not possible for the objectors to put their case directly and hence the need for contacting elected members beforehand. There may be provision for the setting up of public inquiries but, in most cases, this is at the discretion of the local authority.

4.   Road Closures
Proposals to close roads and to divert or close footpaths are put forward under planning legislation (Town and Country Planning (Scotland) Act, 1972) or under the Roads (Scotland) Act 1970 by local highway authorities, and they are advertised in the press. Objections can be made to the Scottish Development Department at New St. Andrew's House and if these are not accepted (or if an acceptable compromise is not reached) an Inquiry may be set up under a Scottish Office Reporter. The final decision will be made by the Secretary of State.

5.   Planning Applications
Most routine planning applications have little serious consequence for cyclists but SPOKES has objected to applications for office building which appear to have a generous provision of car parking space in city centre locations or lack provision for cycle parking whatever the location. Lists of planning applications (the weekly lists) are available with detailed plans at the Planning Department office, Edinburgh District Council, 18 Market Street. Copies of the weekly lists are also sent to organisations — including SPOKES, the Cockburn Association and some community groups. Objections to planning applications will be considered by the Planning Committee of Edinburgh District Council.

As you will have gathered from our comments, SPOKES is far from happy about the adequacy of the various mechanisms of public consultation used in transport planning. It is difficult in many cases to find out what is going on (particularly in detail, for example, when a certain case is coming up before the Committee) and it can be even more difficult to successfully oppose the line taken by the Highways Department. The complexity of the system, its legalistic nature, and the problems of getting your case directly to the councillors who ultimately make the decision, all conspire to maintain the status quo. Nevertheless, SPOKES has found that progress can be made.

SPECIAL MEASURES FOR CYCLISTS

Although it is essential that full account is taken of the needs of cyclists when designing traffic management schemes, road closures and other measures, this alone is unlikely to be sufficient to realise the full potential of cycling as a means of transport in urban areas. Positive measures are also required to implement special measures for cyclists. There is a considerable mythology about the possibility of special measures for cyclists in existing built up areas. Because most of the best facilities are found in some (mainly English) New Towns, there is an uninformed view that special measures are only possible if the whole road network is being designed from scratch. This view is echoed in Lothian Region's Green Paper (June 1978) which states that "it is recognised that the scope will never be as great in an established city centre as in a new suburb or town". Of course this is nonsense. If it is possible to design urban motorways and multi-storey car parks, surely it is possible to cope with cycle-routes and cycle parking racks!   To illustrate what can be done in a city like Edinburgh we have attached 2 maps showing:

(a) some detailed measures that should be considered in the central area;
(b) some outline possibilities that should be considered in the city as a whole.

The maps show only the bare bones of what is possible. The Special measures that are illustrated in this way include:

Bus/Cycle Lanes — We already have these in Edinburgh in some streets and they are of considerable benefit to cyclists. Unfortunately, there are not enough of them. Where there is room but the transport planners consider that a bus lane is not required (either because there is no congestion problem even at rush hours e.g. George IV Bridge, or because they are not used by buses) then a cycle only lane should be provided. Most of the existing bus lanes are too narrow — forcing the cyclist or the bus to move out of the lane to overtake. Where the width of the road makes it possible, the lanes should be widened (the width of the contra flow bus lane in Bread Street is about right). Bus/cycle lanes should also operate throughout the day and not just for limited times at peak periods as at present. Finally, there should be no question of excluding cyclists from any bus lanes — as was initially done in the Bread Street contra-flow cycle lane: this ban on cycles was only removed after a SPOKES campaign.

Priority measures at busy junctions Complex and congested junctions such as Haymarket and Tollcross are a particular problem for cyclists and it is difficult to avoid them. It would be a relatively easy matter at most of the junctions to install special traffic lights which would give cyclists a few seconds priority before cars were allowed through. This would permit cyclists to move safely into the appropriate lane. These "shine through" traffic lights should be accompanied by short cycle lanes on the roads leading up to the junction (for about 100 yards before the junction) to allow cyclists to get to the traffic lights on the inside lane in safety when queues of motor vehicles have formed.

Cyclepaths through parks — SPOKES first campaign was directed at achieving a network of cyclepaths across the Meadows. Depending on the conditions cyclepaths in parks can be segregated from pedestrians or share the same route. Special attention is required with unsegregated cyclepaths and footpaths, but providing that the conditions are right and cyclepaths are carefully designed there is no reason for conflict between pedestrians and cyclists. Apart from the Meadows there are possibilities for cyclepaths in many other parks including Holyrood Park — from St. Leonards Bank to Holyrood Park Road (already lit), Inverleith Park (in both the east/west and north/south direction) and even at the back of Princes Street Gardens where there is a route from Castle Terrace to the Mound, (usually blocked in party by a locked gate near the Floral Clock) which would be ideal for cyclists and is separate from the main footpaths.* Cyclepaths through parks provide an ideal way of avoiding traffic and creating pleasant cycling conditions in urban areas. Experience elsewhere e.g. in Hyde Park in London, has shown that they can be very successful.

Disused rail lines — There is an extensive network of disused rail lines in Edinburgh and they offer, possibly, the most dramatic opportunities for special provision for cyclists in the form of combined walkways/cycleways. There is already one such disused rail line in operation as a walkway and, de facto, cycleway from Balerno to Slateford. Fortunately, there seems to be a real chance for a breakthrough in provision for cyclists in this area over the next few years. Following comments by SPOKES, Edinburgh District Planning Department have agreed that the paths they are developing on the old Leith rail lines from Warriston to Leith and from Easter Road to Seafield and Lochend (see map) should be constructed as combined walkways and cycleways. This work is starting in the summer of 1980 and should be finished in 12 months. It is being paid for by the Scottish Development Agency. The Planning Department also have advanced plans for walkways/cycleways on the disused rail lines between Newbridge and Queensferry and on the Corstorphone line.

In addition to this activity by the District Council Lothian Region, again following comments by SPOKES (in our response to the Green Paper of 1979), have instructed their officials to investigate the feasibility of purchasing and converting all the disused rail lines previously earmarked for roads to walkways/cycleways. £1.2 million has been earmarked for this in the current TPP — for the purchase of the lines and the necessary improvement work. If this goes through the Innocent railway line (South Side to Duddingston) the Roseburn to Davidsons Mains line (with a spur to Granton), the Warriston to Inverleith line and the Trinity to Leith line — see map — should become accessible to cyclists over the next few years. These developments are far from cut and dried — determined lobbying will be required from SPOKES and others to ensure that they go ahead — but there is a reasonable basis for optimism and those concerned in Edinburgh District and Lothian Region are to be congratulated for taking a positive approach to date.

Cyclepaths along canal towpaths — This is an obvious extension of the disused rail line idea. Edinburgh only has one suitable canal — the Union canal — and the towpath has recently been improved to a high standard (although it is rather narrow beyond Harrison Park) linking up with the Colinton-Balerno walkway. If the towpath was extended into the canal basin it could provide an alternative route into the Tollcross area, avoiding

considerable traffic hazards on Gilmore Place and Bruntsfield Road. At present it is technically illegal to cycle on the canal towpath without a permit from the British Waterways Board, and SPOKES believes that this obstruction should be removed particularly during weekday rush hours when bike commuters could use it to avoid heavy traffic and when there are few recreational users. Plans for a walkway along the water of Leith might also provide the opportunity for a combined walkway/cycleway.

Back street cycle routes — A major effort is required to identify back street routes for cyclists which should be closed to through traffic (though not to the vehicles of residents, delivery vehicles etc.) through partial road closures, the use of "sleeping policemen" to reduce traffic speeds and other techniques. We believe that this would be welcomed by the residents of such streets as a considerable improvement to the environment. To date, SPOKES has identified only a limited number of short stretches of road (mainly fitting in with other proposals) for this type of treatment e.g. Tarvit Street and Warrender Park Crescent and Melville Terrace, but there has been little sign of official interest. Edinburgh District and Lothian Region have, however, jointly agreed (following a suggestion by SPOKES) to build a cyclepath along the now closed Dumbiedykes Road from St. Leonards Hill to Viewcraig Gardens, and the work will start in the autumn of 1980. In the long run, back street designated cycle routes offer a major opportunity for extensive improvements for the benefit of cyclists in Edinburgh.

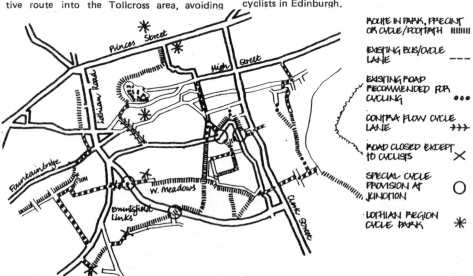

ROUTE IN PARK, PRECINT OR CYCLE/FOOTPATH ||||||

EXISTING BUS/CYCLE LANE ---

EXISTING ROAD RECOMMENDED FOR CYCLING •••

CONTRA FLOW CYCLE LANE >>>

ROAD CLOSED EXCEPT TO CYCLISTS ✗

SPECIAL CYCLE PROVISION AT JUNCTION O

LOTHIAN REGION CYCLE PARK ✳

*This route starts at Castle Terrace and goes along the southern side of the railway line, crossing over the rail line behind the house near the Mound (currently   closed off) and hence avoiding completely the heavily used areas and the steps from the Mound into the Gardens — see map.

7 Controversies

THE UNCONTROLLED CRIME WAVE
by a member of the Scottish Bar

When the Lothians cyclist or pedestrian ventures forth into the street he is entering an environment which police, prosecutors and judges show a remarkable reluctance to control. The cyclist will find left hand lanes blocked by cars illegally parked in contravention of section 477 of the Edinburgh Corporation Order Confirmation Act 1967 which makes it illegal to park a vehicle in any street other than to pick up or set down, he will be at risk from doors carelessly opened in contravention of the Motor Vehicles (Construction and Use) Regulations, and be pursued from behind by other drivers impatiently attempting to overtake when it is unsafe to do so in contravention of section 3 of the Road Traffic Act 1972 which makes it an offence not to show reasonable consideration for other road users. When such vehicles eventually squeeze past they will often travel anything up to ten miles an hour over the legal speed limit, frequently make left turns without signalling, fail to give way to pedestrians and indeed will sometimes crash into each other.

What all such incidents have in common is that the perpetrators enjoy virtual immunity from prosecution: the Chief Constable shrinks from the practical difficulty of dealing with the ubiquitous illegal parking; the procurator fiscal, supported by Crown Office, refuses to prosecute speeding drivers unless they exceed the speed limit by more than ten miles per hour (dismissing as too trivial a crime which increases the stoping distance of a car by around 50 feet); drivers of vehicles which collide causing no serious injury are unlikely to appear in the criminal courts despite the potential danger their carelessness poses for unprotected pedestrians and cyclists; and the police devote little attention to the type of careless or inconsiderate driving examples of which can be witnessed at any pedestrian crossing daily, and which put many more people in a greater state of fear and alarm than the trivial common law breach of the peace which invariably is prosecuted.

To comply with rule 100 of Highway Code a driver turning left should signal and give way to pedestrians crossing the road into which he is turning. Breach of any of the Highway Code rules is a good foundation for a conviction under section 3 of the Road Traffic Act 1972, but this particular breach, although the cause of many serious and fatal accidents, is so seldom prosecuted that a recent report by the British Medical Association deploring the carnage on the roads actually called for it to be made a criminal offence.

The cry at party political and police federation conferences is for 'Law and Order', but it is painfully obvious, particularly to the relatives of the twenty killed and nine hundred injured every day on British roads, that law and order is something to be imposed on the youth who carries a knife, the drunk who swings his fist, or the cashier who dips in the till. Random searches are acceptable if directed at young people walking in the street, but random breath testing for those in charge of a deadly machine is an infringement of individual liberty. No-one calls for "short sharp shocks" for the middle aged drunken motorist.

The killer motorist need fear little if he is convicted. Recent experience shows he will rarely go to prison and the fine may be as low as one hundred pounds. Of course, he will be disqualified from driving for a year or two, and this is supposed to be a severe penalty although it only puts the criminal driver in the same position as half the population, which, because of youth, age, economics or plain common sense, does not drive in any case. (And the disqualified driver can still ride a bicycle!)

The general trend in such sentencing (when the law enacted by Parliament permits a prison sentence of up to five years) reveals a callous disregard by the Scottish shrieval bench for human life and limb where the instrument of injury or destruction is a motor vehicle. And the sheriffs have the full support of the High Court. The excessively lenient sentences of two years and three years respectively meted out by that court in two recent cases involving drunken drivers mounting the pavement and killing, in the one instance, two children, and in the other, three members of a family are a measure of the partiality to be found in even our highest criminal courts. If any other instrument of death had been used the sentences would have been three to four times more severe.

The inadequate handling of motor crime by police and courts arises from two causes, firstly, its enormous incidence, which has swamped the forces of law and order. Every forty mile an hour sign bears testimony to the inability of police and courts to enforce the original thirty mile an hour limit. One of the reasons for allowing the oil crisis speed limits on trunk roads to revert to pre-crisis levels, on the admission of the government of the day, was the inability of the police to enforce the lower limits (which had contributed not only to fuel conservation but also to road safety).

Secondly, the forces of law and order, police, prosecutors and judges are largely motorists and many of them appear unable to bring a disinterested approach to bear on motoring crime: while such attitudes persist no pedestrian or cyclist can use the public thoroughfare with any guarantee of safety.

IS THE CAR A DRUG?
by Evan Lloyd

The motor car has become such an ubiquitous item of urban furniture that it is often forgotten that the original concept of a car was as a replacement for the horse as a means of transport, and in this its prime function it has become very valuable especially in isolated areas, for groups, families and for some physically disabled people. Unfortunately, secondary uses have developed. Among some groups the car is used as a status symbol indicating the relative ranking of a person or family in the pecking order, the more numerous newer, faster, larger or more expensive the car the higher the status of the person or family or the assumed success of the business. A subcult identified the car as a virility symbol. This may range from the mere possession of any vehicle by a young man, to the ownership of a 'sports job' as money or age increase. The young thugs who steal cars for 'joy-riding' are possibly trying to establish a virility status with their girl or gang. Businesses have also developed the use of the car as a means of tax reduction or avoidance or as a hidden pay rise.

The car, however, has some serious side effects in society. With approximately a quarter of a million people injured in road accidents in Britain every year, physical injury associated with the motor car has reached epidemic proportions and for any individual the result may range from minor grazes to death, or brain damage leaving a tragic semi-vegetable state. The immediate care cost the country £85,000,000 in 1975 but this figure is dwarfed by the cost of long-term care and the social and personal consequences of this carnage.

One problem is that people become addicted to the motor car and if anyone doubts this they have only to think back to the occurrences in California when petrol suddenly became in short supply. There were shootings and stabbings, and women were prepared to prostitute themselves in order to obtain petrol (behaviour more usually associated with addiction to hard drugs like heroin). The addition may take several forms. The speed addict requires to drive as fast as possible with no regard for risk to himself or others, even in dangerous conditions; e.g. narrow twisting roads, side roads

where children play, ungritted ice or motorway fog, and if the traffic is heavy the speed addict will twist and turn along side roads even although the total time saved may only be a few seconds. This addiction is also manifested in a desire for cars which have a greater top speed and/or acceleration. The speed addict is pandered to by planners and administrators, the objective seeming to be to enable cars to travel as fast and with as few delays as possible ignoring the requirements of pedestrians, cyclists, and users of public transport.

Another manifestation of addiction to the motor car is physical inactivity. The addict has become so used to the car that he will insist on using it on every occasion without thought of time, e.g. over short distances, the time taken to get the car out of a garage and to the destination and parked may be longer than the time taken to walk the same distance.

There are other psychological effects. The personality change, where normally quiet, retiring people become very aggressive and over-assertive when they enter a car has become so common that it has become a subject for cartoons. Manners are also affected, car drivers behaving to other road users with a lack of courtesy which may be completely out of character. The effect is proportional to the size, newness, speed potential or opulence of the car. Motorists also repeatedly flout the laws with a self-righteous lack of guilt, particularly with regard to speed limits, traffic lights, parking regulations, bus lanes or alcohol. If caught, they react by criticising the police for having nothing better to do, and expect sympathy for having been caught. The same people however, expect youngsters to obey the law implicitly.

Car driving produces stress which may be implicated in mental illness and gastro-intestinal problems, and people who cannot cope resort to the excessive consumption of tranquillisers or other forms of pills, or food (contributing to obesity), excessive smoking or increased consumption of alcohol. The inactivity resulting from driving, often combined with stress is frequently implicated in the causation of other medical problems which contribute significantly to industrial inefficiency and absenteeism, e.g. backache.

In the environment the motor car may cause physical damage from direct impact or vibration; air pollution from fumes including carbon monoxide and lead; physical pollution from moving and parked vehicles; and noise. A less obvious environmental hazard is that of social damage. Communities can be destroyed either with heavy through traffic or by an excessive use of cars, resulting in personal isolation, e.g. in tenement areas in towns, people used to walk in the streets or speak to each other from the windows. Traffic has made this impossible and the tenement residents, especially the elderly, become cut off. Also in dormitory suburbs young wives with young children can be very isolated because of the high proportion of people who drive to work to shop etc. It is interesting that most of the active community groups are located in areas with a low density of car ownership.

The car, like cancer, is spreading, metastasising and threatening to destroy its human host. Certainly many drugs with fewer dangers have been banned or placed on a number of schedules which necessitate a prescription for use.

Even Lloyd is Consultant Anaesthetist at Princess Margaret Rose Hospital and a member of SPOKES

Reprinted by kind permission of 'Edinburgh Medicine'.

OFFICIALS AND COUNCILLORS –
WHO DECIDES WHAT HAPPENS?

The Recent History and Politics of Planning for Cyclists in Edinburgh

Edinburgh has been fortunate in avoiding much of the dereliction which has been visited on many other cities by the growth in numbers of the private motor car. Vigorous campaigning by community, amenity and environmental organisations, together with public expenditure cuts and years of indecision by the old Edinburgh Corporation, and finally the more enlightened and egalitarian transport policies of the new Regional Council, have resulted in the cancellation in 1978 of the old Inner Ring Roadplans and, in 1979, of the threatened inner city approach roads which would have brought A1/M8/M9 traffic right to the heart of the city.

OVERALL TRANSPORT POLICIES

Shortly before Labour was elected to the control of the Region in April 1978 they told SPOKES: *"Our policy is, in conjunction with an outer bypass, progressively to restrict private vehicle penetration into the central area and to create conditions which, by limiting the total volume of private and commercial traffic in the city, are suitable for public transport, pedestrians and cyclists"*. This policy is not one which is liked by all councillors – and it is certainly not ideal as far as some senior officials of the road-engineer dominated Highways Department (appropriately named "highways" rather than "transport") are concerned. The Director, Mr. Alexander Crockett, still thinks wistfully of the old inner ring road plans. Not long ago he told a member of SPOKES what excellent conditions for pedestrians and cyclists could have been created within this inner ring had it been built — through Queen Street, under the West End, through Tollcross, over the Meadows (on stilts in one plan!), the Pleasance, under the High Street, and back over the end of Waverley to the top of Leith Walk.

More recently, officials very strongly supported the proposed Eastern and Western approach roads, arguing that if they were built then better conditions for pedestrians, cyclists and public transport could be created on the "relevied" roads. These arguments were wholeheartedly supported by Conservative and Liberal councillors, and also initially by some Labour councillors. It was only after a major public consultation exercise, which showed overwhelming public opposition, that the decision to scrap the roads and stick to the policy on which they had been elected was agreed by Labour councillors. SPOKES, through its Planning Group, played a major part in this exercise. The group drew up a detailed discussion paper (now on sale as a SPOKES report, "Transportation in the Edinburgh Area") which was circulated to all SPOKES members, all councillors, and many residents and community organisations. Certainly, there was little dissention within SPOKES, with only one member coming back to tell us that they disagreed with our submission. However, the plans for these roads remain in Highway Department filing cabinets, and there is little doubt that they could be resurrected and dusted off should the opportunity arise again in the future.

POLICIES FOR CYCLISTS

As far as provision for cyclists specifically is concerned, the policy of the Regional Council is now a very positive one. The original version of the Lothian Region Structure Plan (which deals with land use and transport policies for the 1980's) had nothing to say about provision for cyclists, and even failed to mention walking as a means of getting to work! (although almost a quarter of the journeys to work in Lothian are by foot). However, following an appearance by SPOKES in 1978 at the Examination in Public of the Structure Plan, the Council and the Secretary of State both agreed that the Plan be amended as SPOKES had suggested — see inset.

WHAT HAPPENS IN PRACTICE

Despite this policy, however, consideration for cyclists in practice in transport planning is grossly inadequate. The reason for this appears to be twofold. Firstly, Highways officials are not particularly interested in cyclists — road engineers are trained to build roads, and that is what they prefer to do. Even traffic management specialists seem to think largely in terms of motor traffic. Secondly, although councillors have a policy to favour cyclists (along with pedestrians and public transport) few councillors are cyclists themselves, and with the very many calls on their time they do not exert the necessary muscle to see that their policies are converted into practice. Even though a few token schemes for cyclists are introduced there is no general consideration for the needs of cyclists in the day to day work of the council. Unless cyclists, as individuals as well as through SPOKES, keep up a consistent pressure on the councillors, we can expect little major progress. These two reasons explain why the Structure Plan didn't mention cyclists until SPOKES intervened; why the promise by councillors in December 1978 to install experimental cycle parking in the city centre had still not been carried out by officials at the time of writing (October 1980) although in the same period hundreds of cycle parking places had been installed in other local authorities; why virtually no special measures for cyclists have been put forward by the council; and why, without one exception cyclists have been ignored in all new road and traffic management plans (see "Planning" chapter for many examples).

The several small steps for cyclists which have been achieved through the Regional

Council (with the one major exception of the council's proposed cycleway along Middle Meadow Walk) have come when SPOKES has been able to put a spanner in the official works. Many schemes for road and traffic management have by law to be advertised to the public for objections (see "Planning" chapter), and the SPOKES Planning Group has taken every opportunity to speak up for cyclists on these occasions. Such objections have to be answered by the officials, and the objections have to be reported to the councillors.

Moreover, the objection has to be dealt with to the satisfaction of the councillors or the Secretary of State before the scheme in question can go ahead. This is how we got provision for cyclists in the McEwan Hall precinct, the Dumbiedykes cycle route, permission for cyclists to use the Bread Street contra-flow bus lane, the Lady Lawson Street contra-flow cycle lane, and many lesser successes.

DIFFICULTIES FOR OBJECTORS

Although this procedure for objecting to official plans does give the public a chance, it is still fraught with pitfalls, and all the cards are stacked against the objector. The councillors only see summaries, drawn up by the officials, of objections — although councillors may of course ask to see the full statement. The officials also have the last word since objectors are not given any opportunity to see or comment on the officials' report on their objections. Councillors themselves only receive the papers a few days before the relevant meeting. Furthermore it is very difficult for an outsider (unless they have a lot of time to spare and access to a phone during office hours) to find out which meeting of which Council committee will be considering a particular matter, so as to be able to speak to councillors beforehand to ask for an opportunity to appear in person.

Can the procedure really be so difficult for the member of the public to influence? The story of the Lady Lawson Street contra-flow cycle lane provides some interesting insights. After 18 months of detailed submissions and reasoned argument by SPOKES to the effect that considerable numbers of cyclists were inconvenienced, and that many were virtually forced to perform dangerous or illegal manoeuvres, by the new traffic management scheme in the area, officials finally presented our case to a meeting of the Highways Sub-Committee. We were not informed officially when this was going to happen. Had it not been for the fact that we had already discussed the matter in detail with a councillor on that committee on a number of occasions, the committee would almost certainly have been misled by the report from the officials. Instead of estimating the number of cyclists likely to use a contra-flow lane, the report stated the number counted travelling from east to west in Bread Street. One might as well decide whether to build a road to London by counting the number of cars leaving Edinburgh for Aberdeen! The count in Bread Street (which totalled 3!) was the *only* figure in the report, which also contained various other misleading or innaccurate assertions. Fortunately the councillor with whom we had previously discussed the matter (Cllr. William Roe, Holyrood/Meadows) read the report in advance of the committee and found the difference between our story and that of the officials so remarkable that he went to Lady Lawson Street himself in the morning rush hour and spent an hour counting passing cyclists. The results were so convincing that he was able to persuade every member of the committee, whatever their political complexion, to vote down the officials' report and go ahead with the contra-flow cycle lane on an experimental basis.

Although the procedures for public consultation and objections do give cyclists some chance to influence the decision making process, the results are rarely fully satisfactory for two further reasons. Firstly objections are piecemeal responses to individual proposals as they come up, and there is no coherent overall plan for cycle provision. The Dumbiedykes cycle route, for example, was obtained by objecting to a road closure order. However, because the route was dealt with in complete isolation the obvious possibilities for linking it to many nearby generators of cycle traffic were all missed — despite repeated comment and protest by SPOKES. Near to the cycle route are the University Sports Centre and lecture rooms, proposed new student residences, proposed new SSHA housing, the Commonwealth Pool, the Pollock Halls of residence, and Southside shopping and residential area, and the disused railway line to Craigmillar. Yet none of these possibilities appears to have received any real consideration; and many cyclists who could have used the route will still be forced to use the fast, heavily-trafficked, steep and cobbled main road through the Pleasance or make a long detour. This lack of adequate planning is all the more surprising in the light of the government manual "Ways of Helping Cyclists in Built Up Areas" (which although not officially applicable in Scotland still contains much relevant material), which states: *"the identification of major generators and attractors of cycle traffic will need to be obtained ... From this information the patterns of desire lines for cycle trips can be established"*, and so on. More generally there are now several definite plans for provision for cyclists in the Southside area. These include the Dumbiedykes scheme, the McEwan Hall precinct, the Middle Meadow Walk scheme, cycle parking in Chambers Street; in addition to some other possible schemes. Despite this, no overall plan has been drawn up on provision for cyclists, within which these schemes can be put into perspective. SPOKES made one such proposal in 1978 in "Cycling in the Southside", our submission on the Southside Local Plan, but this has never been taken up by Highways officials. Thus individual schemes go ahead in an arbitrary and ad-hoc way, making a mockery of sensible long-term planning. This is reflected in the ad-hoc nature of the comments on cycling in the draft Southside Local Plan. The second related problem is that the schemes for cyclists which do go ahead are not necessarily those which should have the greatest priority. Taking the Dumbiedykes scheme again, this would not have been considered an early priority by SPOKES in an overall scheme of cycle provision. However, since the Council was doing nothing for cyclists, and had no priorities regarding such provision, SPOKES had to take every opportunity to influence events as they presented themselves.

THE IMPORTANCE OF OFFICIALS

Returning to the theme of the importance of the attitudes of council officials, there is an interesting contrast between progress on cycle provision by the Regional and District Councils. The Regional Council has a clear commitment to provision for cyclists — and indeed to *"encourage more people to walk and cycle for work and leisure purposes"* — and this commitment was one of the policies with which Labour was elected to control of the Region in 1978. The District Council, on the other hand (although many members in all parties are sympathetic to the needs of cyclists) does not have any clear commitment one way or the other: the practice of the Conservatives (who control the District Council) is generally to decide on issues as they come up rather than being elected with more than an outline manifesto. Despite this difference, the District Council has already started work on two walkway/cycleways (Warriston/Coburg and Easter Road/Seafield) and has two more (Corstorphine/Balgreen and Queensferry/Newbridge) under detailed investigation, whilst the Region has got nothing on the ground specifically for cyclists apart from three small signs allowing cyclists to use the Bread Street contra-flow bus lane.

The explanation for these differences does not appear too hard to find. The officials in the District Planning Department take a sympathetic interest in the needs of cyclists and pedestrians as a major priority, and so they put forward positive proposals which the councillors are naturally happy to go along with where funds can be found. Officials in the Regional Highways Department, on the other hand, are mainly interested in roads and motor traffic. Thus they do not present initiatives to councillors on cycle provision, and when they respond to other people's ideas they are not enthusiastic and do not look imaginatively at the possibilities. One further example of the importance of the officials can be mentioned, indicating also that this is not a question of "District versus Region". Some senior officials in the District Recreation department are not very happy about the idea of a Meadows cycleway (although as far as we know most District councillors have not — by August 1980 — taken up strong positions either for or against — and certainly the Council itself has not). This has resulted in serious hold-ups for the main scheme promised by the Region to cyclists — the Middle Meadow Walk cycleway.

The conclusion is by no means an unusual one. Councillors are very busy people. They will naturally go along with the recommendations of their expert officials unless they have very good reasons not to; and they will be reluctant to instruct officials to do other things, and to make sure that they do them in a reasonable time. Only by determined and continual lobbying of councillors by cyclists as individuals as well as through cycling organisations will major advances be made. So — when did you last phone up your councillor, visit his or her surgery, or even write? Please turn to the appendix for their phone numbers.

LOTHIAN REGIONAL COUNCIL POLICY ON WALKING AND CYCLING
"The Regional Council will co-operate with the District Councils to implement schemes that will allow greater freedom of movement to pedestrians and cyclists, and encourage more people to walk and cycle for work and leisure journeys".

There was a bureaucrat from the Scottish Office who took up cycling for his health after many years of motoring. It was all right the first day, and when he got home he rode the bike into the garage and shut the door as usual. But the next morning, he had to give up cycling. He couldn't find reverse gear to get the damn thing out!

SAVE TIME
SAVE MONEY BE FIT FOR LIFE
SAVE PETROL

8 Leisure

HOLIDAYS FOR THE CYCLIST
By Dave du Feu

The urban cyclist who has never ventured further out of Edinburgh than Musselburgh or Cramond is a rapidly increasing species, as more people take to cycling as a cheap and convenient method of commuting or shopping. If you are one of these — as I was until 3 years ago — you will come back ecstatic from your first cycling holiday.

Just imagine it!!! No glass on the roads (but beware of clippings from hawthorn hedges!); cross-country tracks from which motor traffic is banned; quiet mountain roads or country lanes where you can go for hours without hearing a car (and when one does eventually pass the driver will be the type who gives you a cheery smile); free-wheeling downhill for miles without once having to pedal; and the chance to be really grateful for that extra-large sprocket you asked for on the back wheel. Above all the feeling of freedom and the great unpolluted outdoors.

The main point of this section is to tell you where to find out more: and we'll make a point of mentioning those local authorities and organisations who are beginning to do something for holidaying cyclists. Edinburgh and Lothian, regrettably, cannot yet be included. The addresses of everything in italic type appear at the end.

What to take

There are three main kinds of bike holiday. Most advanced, most dedicated, and most free is bicycle camping — "bikepacking" as it is known. Beginners are strongly advised to read, *"Bikepacking for Beginners"*. The book is well-illustrated and it will ensure that you take everything you do need and — more important! — that you won't take anything you don't need. The only failings of the book are that the cyclist in most of the photos look exceedingly grim and that it makes bikepacking look like an all-male pursuit (is this why he looks so grim?). Not a single cyclist in the book is female, and the author thanks his wife, "who keeps the home fires burning".

The second type of holiday is where you don't take a tent, and you stay at youth hostels or bed-and-breakfasts. If you're a CTC member, take the *CTC Handbook* with you — it's full of B & Bs who've been recommended by other cyclists and from personal experience a recommended B & B is often a good one.

Finally, you can stay at a fixed point, and cycle from it. The advantage, obviously, is that your bike is very much lighter. Try renting a cottage or caravan in the middle of some wild country, and you can spend a delightful week exploring by bike and on foot.

As to what to take — the *CTC Route Guide* has a helpful appendix on clothes and tools and *Bikepacking for Beginners* is useful even if you are not bikepacking. But one word of warning — do not take a rucksack. The only real must about cycletouring is the necessity for some reasonably good panniers and a pannier rack. If money is a problem, the July 1980 issue of *Freewheeling* magazine tells you how to make your own.

Travelling

It won't take you many hours to get out of Edinburgh into Midlothian and then the Borders, but if you want to go further afield take advantage of British Rail's free bikes-by-train scheme. At the time of writing bikes are banned on Eastern Region 125s, but SPOKES and other groups are hoping to get this ban modified. In any case, this still

leaves free bike travel on the vast majority of BR's remaining network. A free leaflet *"Taking Your Cycle by Train"* is available.

One very pleasurable nearby holiday is around the islands off the west coast. These holidays are especially attractive to cyclists because Caledonian MacBrayne shipping, who operate island ferries, have introduced ridiculously low charges for bicycles (see advert). In addition they sell "Rover" tickets for the cyclist (but not for the bike). These at present (August 1980) cost £18 for 8 days or £26 for 15 days.

Maps and Routes

For planning your holiday try the Ordnance Survey 1:250,000 maps. But assuming you want to find the really quiet roads and tracks it is essential to take detailed maps.

Probably the best value for money (for the cyclist) are the Bartholomews 1:100,000 series. If you can afford more — and especially if you are having a "fixed point" holiday — take the Ordnance Survey 1:50,000 maps. A useful map within Scotland is the Touring Map published by the Scottish Tourist Board (scale 5 miles = 1 inch), which includes sites of interest to tourists.

Several imaginative local authorities have now brought out route guides for cyclists. Most unusual is the *Cumbria Cycle Way* leaflet, which describes a 250-mile circular tour sticking very largely to quiet roads and passing through delightful countryside of several different types. Nearer home Tayside Regional Council has brought out a booklet, *"Tayside — Cycling"* which describes a whole range of tours for cyclists — from 10 to 150 miles — including not only quiet roads but "roughstuff" country tracks. If, incidentally, you think Lothian could do something like this please write to The Convener of the Recreation and Leisure Committee, Lothian Regional Council, Parliament Square, Edinburgh 1.

Local authorities are not the only bodies who can produce route guides. Our fellow campaign group in Bristol and Avon, Cyclebag, has a number of route maps on sale. They have too built their own cycle-route on a disused railway line between Bath and Bristol — and a bicycle hire centre is now operating on the route. In London, Friends of the Earth and the London Cycling Campaign have produced *"On Your Bike"*. This includes a reprint of 20 pages of the London A—Z map with recommended safer routes for cyclists over-printed in red. This will be useful if you decide to go to London for a business trip or an urban holiday. But at present the Route Guide of all Route Guides is the mammoth *"CTC Route Guide to Cycling in Britain and Ireland"*. This contains 365 routes, "interconnected to form an intricate pattern over the British Isles", so that they can be linked to form holidays of any desired length. It must be used in conjunction with detailed maps such as those listed above, and because of its weight it is probably more useful for planning your holiday than actually taking with you — you can always photocopy the relevant pages.

One final word — I have mentioned "planning your route". Personally, it seems more fun to do no advance planning other than decide the general area where you are going. That much is essential, so that you can buy the right maps, look up the relevant guides such as those mentioned above, and decide which of your friends and relatives to visit (or avoid). After that — leave your detailed planning for each day till the night before, and be ready to change your plans en route when your nose leads you somewhere.

Addresses for items mentioned above

(1) **Bikepacking for Beginners** R Adshead (Oxford Illustrated Press), on sale in shops or from CTC Sales, 69 Meadrow, Godalming, Surrey, GU7 3HS.

(2) **Youth Hostels** handbook on sale to members from Scottish Youth Hostels Association, 161 Warrender Park Road, Edinburgh EH9 1EQ. 031-229 8660.

(3) **CTC Handbook** on sale to members from (1).

(4) **CTC Route Guide to Cycling in Britain and Ireland** on sale from (1).

(5) **Freewheeling** magazine on sale from 14 Picardy Place, Edinburgh 1. 031-557 0718

(6) **Taking Your Cycle by Train** free from The Chief Passenger Manager, British Rail (Scotland), Buchanan House, Glasgow G4 OHG. 041-332 9811 ext. 3731.

(7) **Caledonian MacBrayne**, The Ferry Terminal, Gourock, PA19 1QP. 0475-33755.

(8) **Ordnance Survey** maps on sale from Sustainable Transport, 35 King Street, Bristol BS1 4DZ. 0272-28893.

(9) **Scottish Tourist Board Touring Map** on sale from 23 Ravelston Terrace, Edinburgh EH4 3EU.

(10) **Cumbria Cycleway** leaflet free from Cumbria Tourist Board, Ellerthwaite, Windermere, Cumbria.

(11) **Tayside — Cycling** on sale from Tourist Officer, Tayside Regional Council, 28 Crichton Street, Dundee DD1 3RD.

(12) **On Your Bike** on sale from SPOKES

(13) **Cyclebag** maps on sale from (8).

There once was a member of SPOKES
Who was told to think up cycling jokes
He sat up all night
Until by daylight
He decided there weren't any, because cycling is basically an intensely serious matter.

BIKE GAMES
By Robert Smith of SPOKES Events Group

If you like fun and using your bike, but don't feel up to the Tour de France then SPOKES have produced some games just for you. Most of the games can be played on grass or tarmac although grass is probably safer. A length of ground about 50 yards long is all that is needed. The first five games are competitive and the remainder not, but all give much amusement to spectators and particpants alike.

(1) **Spanner Race** Participants will require a spanner and possibly a pump. Start by cycling to one end, remove the front wheel when you get there and take it back to the start. Then do the same with the frame. The idea now is to re-assemble your bike as quickly as possible and cycle to the finishing line. If your bike has quick release wheels then you should also deflate the tyres when you take the wheels off.

(2) **Slow Race** This is self-explanatory really! No stopping, no putting your feet down, no zig-zagging. The last person across the finishing line wins.

(3) **Balloon Race** Cyclists compete in pairs holding a balloon between the palms of their hands. Cycle to the far end and turn round, without dismounting.. The first pair back wins.

(4) **Blindfold race** Cyclists put buckets on their heads. They are allocated a guide who follows behind. They are guided to the far end and back — everyone will need plenty of room.

(5) **Freewheeling Competition** Each cyclist is given a set length of road to build up speed and then they must stop pedalling. Whoever then freewheels the furthest is the winner.

(6) **Crossover Arm Cycling** Put the right hand on the left handlebar, the left hand on the right handlebar. Now try to weave between a line of bollards and back to the start without putting your feet down.

(7) **Bicycle Shapes** Lean three bicycles together to form a triangle, now try to form a square, five for a pentagon, ten cycles can form a circle, a figure of eight, a star or a straight line. The Bristol group, Cyclebag, formed a 150 bicycle circle in which participants lay to form spokes for a photograph. SPOKES tried it in 1979 but couldn't get the whole circle to stay up!

The Blindfold Game, (SPOKES Annual Rally May 1980)

FORTH BRIDGES DAY TOUR
By Peter Teague
(INCLUDING DOLLAR AND THE CLEISH HILLS)

The intention of this tour is to combine frequent rail services with the use of the maximum of quiet and scenic routes available. There are, however, one or two steep hills, mainly in the road around Dollar.

Train to FALKIRK Grahamston Station.

Turn first left on leaving station, through car park and left at Post Office. Follow B905 to Carron and turn left (S.P. Kincardine Bridge) onto B9036; Follow to Carronshore and turn right at crossroads. In ½m. turn right just before "Millar's Truck Rental" Proceed over bridge over M9 to join with A905. Turn right.

Follow A905 to roundabout joining A876 (S.P. Kincardine Bridge) — Cyclepath!. At Kincardine Bridge best to use footpath (heavy lorries). Continue to Kincardine.

In town, turn left at crossroads opposite Clock Tower and in ¾m turn left onto road marked "Unsuitable for Motor Vehicles". In a few yards turn left again then right (Chapelhill Road) and proceed over railway bridge with Power Station on left. Under power lines arriving at CLACKMANNAN.

In town, turn right at Clock Tower and in ¼m join B910 at "Give Way". Pass over one railway, under A907 and under Alloa-Dunfermline railway to join A977.

Turn left and proceed to Forest Mill to turn left (S.P. Coalsnaughton). In 1m (2 steepish hills) turn right onto B9140, then (in ½m) left. Steep downward gradient (1 in 7) for ½m to join B913. Turn left and in ¾m, reach DOLLAR.

There is an attractive walk up the Dollar Glen path and Castle Campbell (National Trust/Department of Environment) is worth a visit being attractively set with a promontory between two gorges. Access to the Ochils, e.g. White Wisp Hill from just above Castle.

Leave Dollar eastwards on A91 and turn right (S.P. Pitgober, Blairingone). Decend hill.

After Vicar's Bridge turn sharp left uphill past disused railway to join A977. (Minor road, quite steep though attractive. Could avoid by detour via Rumbling Bridge and Powmill).

Turn left onto A977 (fairly busy route — some lorries) as far as Powmill. Turn right onto A823.

In 1½m, at AA box, turn sharp left for Cleish. Follow road along scarp side of Cleish Hills. ¼m beyond Cleish turn right.

A stiff climb now ensues via Nivingston, skirting Loch Glow and Blairadam Forest to join B914. Turn left for KELTY.

In Kelty take B912 (S.P. Cowdenbeath, Dunfermline) by turning right. In ¾m beyond Kelty, at foot of hill turn left (for INVERKEITHING) onto B917.

Proceed via Hill of Beath onto A910 and CROSSGATES. At traffic lights carry straight on (B961: A.P. Inverkeithing) for 3m to join with A92 (S.P. Dunfermline or Kirkcaldy). Turn right to cross railway, then immediately left onto B981 again to enter INVERKEITHING. (38 Miles).

In ¼m turn left for railway station (or proceed to Forth Road Bridge. Direct route to Edinburgh (14 miles).

Note: route via Cleish with its steep hills can be avoided by continuing along the A823 to the B914 and then turning left for Kelty.

Did you know that Tennyson warned his readers that British, French or German bikes were better than cheap Hong Kong imports? He wrote "Better fifty years of Europe than a cycle of Cathay." (If you don't believe me, check *Locksley Hall,* line 184.)

TOUR THROUGH PENTLAND HILLS   by Peter Teague

This tour uses disused rail routes, hill tracks and as many quiet roads as possible. The part of the route through the Hills is not cycleable and has several styles to cross, so single travellers might find it difficult, also light bikes would be an advantage. There are also steep hills near Bonnyrigg.

Leave Edinburgh by the A701 (S.P. Peebles). At 2m. from North Bridge (the foot of Liberton Brae) turn left opposite the entrance to Braid Hills Road (by shops) and go up Kirk Brae and continue along main road for the next 1½m; crossing A720 and entering Midlothian District, then descending the hill to join A768. (S.P. Dalkeith). Continue to Bonnyrigg. (6 miles).

Cross River North Esk and about 100 yds up hill take sharp right turn. Proceed up hill through Polton towards Rosewell. 200 yds after Hawthornden turn right and continue (with remains of railway line and council estate on left) to junction with B7003. (8¾ miles).

Turn right and at the next corner turn left onto a cinder track. This is what remains of the railway line from Eskbank, through Auchendinny to Penicuik. There are two parallel tracks — take the track on the right. The surface is fairly good, occasionally muddy and the undergrowth is occasionally close. Continue for two miles. (10¾ miles).

After crossing viaduct proceed through tunnel (unlighted). Take path to the right of Dalmore Mill and emerge on the road in front of another tunnel. Do NOT enter tunnel, but turn right up the hill to crossroads (junction with B7026). (11 miles).

Straight across crossroads and continue up hill. View emerges of viaduct on right, (railway from Roslin to Penicuik). In ½m. cross A766 and continue for 1½m. to junction with A702. (13 miles). Turn right.

At bottom of the hill, turn sharp left for Flotterstone Inn. Proceed up Glencorse past Glencorse and Loganlea Reservoirs to the "Home". (16¾ miles).

After going through gate cross right over Logan Burn. Follow west flank of Black Hill until path reaches wire fence with metal stile. Cross stile and bear left through valley until muddy stream bridged by planks is reached. (Signpost: "Keep to Right of Way").

Cross stream by fence. Follow path round to left. Cross Wooden stile and make for gate on left end of belt of trees. (Bavelaw Castle). (19 miles).

Climb stile and take road downhill, crossing Threipmuir Reservoir by causeway. Proceed along main road through Balerno (pass Mallery House on right). (22 miles).

On emerging onto A70 turn right, look for gap in the wall on right side of road. This is the entrance to the former Balerno-Slateford Railway — now a footpath. This can be followed in connection with the canal towpath as far as Fountainbridge, (emerge Gilmore Park). At present the track is indistinct when passing under the viaduct of the new Outer City By-Pass. (28 miles).

*   *Route number 3 in Bartholemew's Pentland Hills Map.*

DID YOU KNOW THAT ...

(a) Tandems are now so popular that two people are riding a tandem for every one riding a bike.

(b) The reason so many cyclists are late for work is that their bikes are two tyred.

A SHORT TOUR IN EAST LOTHIAN   By Nick Marshall

A cycle trip in East Lothian will always reward you handsomely for the effort expended. It is a beautiful county with rolling countryside, gentle slopes, fine views, and many quiet country lanes. This is a 2—3 hour (25 miles) trip with only moderate hills.

OUTWARD

Start by taking a scenic pedal through HOLYROOD PARK and continuing through DUDDINGSTON VILLAGE. Turn RIGHT on leaving the village and follow Duddingston Road West for a mile as it pleasantly skirts the east end of Duddingston Loch and passes through some of the less scenic parts of Craigmillar.

Turn LEFT at the first set of traffic lights, where S. Luca's ice-cream shop sits on the opposite corner. This road will lead you all the way to MUSSELBURGH, where you turn RIGHT at the traffic lights to get back on to the A1. It goes through the town, over the bridge, and makes a sharp left turn and on through more town. A hundred metres after the bridge, turn RIGHT, following a sign to INVERESK. More signs direct you to this village, which is old and beautiful, and a National Trust property.

. If you can drag yourself away, keep on up the peaceful country road (A6124), which crosses a roundabout (follow signs for Pathhead) and starts to ascend a long hill. Rising slowly above the coastal plain, you may look over your shoulder at an interesting panorama stretching from the Pentlands to Fife.

The road continues along for a mile and rises to a crossroads, where you turn RIGHT, go over the railway bridge (the disused railway underneath runs to Pencaitland, and is well worth walking along. Although it's a bit overgrown here, the section from Ormiston to Pencaitland has been made into a cycle/walkway).

Turn LEFT directly after the bridge. This road, which is still heading towards Pathhead, passes two green telephone boxes before entering a wooded dell where old mining skips, brightly painted, are displayed. Here you may turn LEFT following a sign for Cousland, and go up a steep, short slope, with old limekilns near the top.

Turn LEFT at the top of the hill, into COUSLAND, which is a picturesque hilltop town. Continuing on this road, you will find fine views over most of East Lothian.

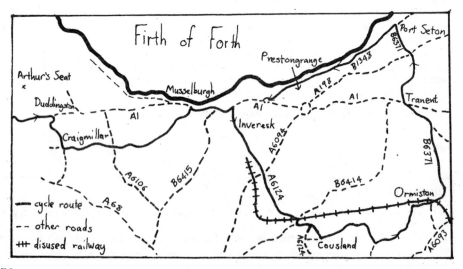

72

After gliding down the road, turn LEFT at the T-junction and on along a tree-lined lane to the pleasant village of ORMISTON.

RETURN

For a change of scenery, take the B6371 to Tranent, and through this town towards Cockenzie and Port Seton. This is mostly downhill and affords many wide panoramas over the Forth.

At PORT SETON, turn LEFT along the coast road (B1384), passing Prestongrange Beam Engine and other relics of the steam age as you approach MUSSELBURGH. Almost any road from Musselburgh takes you, by hook or crook, back to Auld Reekie.

There are many other pleasant country roads through the varying East Lothian landscape, but I would advise you to generally keep off A roads and avoid the A1 at all costs, as drivers go like a bomb. They don't know what they're missing. Do note, though, that the wind usually comes from the West, so avoid pedalling back into town along the coast roads, and perhaps catching a chill, on windy days.

CYCLISTS' BOOKSHELF
by Ian Maxwell

Many books have been written on topics relating to cycling — most libraries contain a fair selection — but only a few are worth seeking out. This selection is a personal choice of what I find interesting, useful or simply enjoyable. Some worthwhile books have certainly been omitted and many remain to be published. Many publishers have a cycling book in preparation at the moment.

Where a book is not readily available, an address is given for the publisher. Most of these volumes can be obtained from the CTC Bookshop, 69 Meadrow, Godalming, Surrey GU7 3HS, or Selpress Books, 16 Berkely Street, London W1X 6AP. Tel: 0425 618663.

1. Transport, planning and campaigning

Transport and town planning is a vast topic, although much of the literature is concerned with improving the flow of motor vehicles. *"Instead of Cars"* by Terence Bendixson, (Pelican, 1977) is an extremely readable introduction to this topic from the opposite point of view. Walking, cycling and public transport are discussed in depth. The same can be said of the excellent, more recent, book *Taming Traffic* by Stephen Plowden (Andre Deutsch, 1980).

Vital Travel Statistics by Mick Hamer and Stephen Potter (Transport 2000, 40 James Street, London 1979, 24 pp) contains 20 annotated tables of statistics. It helps to sort out the arguments on the levels of usage of various forms of transport.

The Bicycle Planning Book, edited by Mike Hudson (Open Books/FoE, 1978, 154 pp), contains chapters on transport usage statistics, safety, law, planning and design of facilities. Although an essential reference source, a new edition would be useful to keep up to date with changes in the law.

A less academic, more down-to-earth approach is evident from the title of *Way Ahead — the Bicycle Warriors Handbook,* by Mike Hudson (FoE, 9 Poland Street, London, 1979). This explains how to go about organising and running a bicycle campaign.

Finally there is *Energy and Equity* by Ivan Illich. Illich, in his inimitable but slightly obscure style, concludes that the bicycle is the ideal form of transport. See 'Publications for Bike Campaigners' in *Freewheeling* magazine Dec. 1979 p 27 for more books in this category.

2 Technical handbooks

Two maintenance books are outstanding, and although both have weaknesses, together they are very worthwhile.

Everyone should be able to afford the Readers Digest Basic Guide *"The Maintenance of Bicycles and Mopeds* (40 pp), and it will not break the bank to buy *Richard's Bicycle Book* by Richard Ballantine (Pan, 1979, 383 pp). Richard's book also contains a great deal of advice about all aspects of cycling, and is very readable. He does not hesitate to express his opinions forcibly, and has changed his mind on a few topics (such as helmets for cyclists!) since the first edition came out.

A technical explanation of the physics and mathematics of cycling is found in *Bicycling Science* by F. R. Whitt and D. G. Wilson (MT Press, 1974, hardback and paperback). This books is hard work, but worth making an effort to read. A new and larger edition is being prepared.

Pedal Power in Work, Leisure and Transportation (ed James C. McCullagh, Rodale Press, 1977, 133 pp) is a collection of items about the use of pedal power in various forms.

3. Touring and leisure

Many guides to cycletouring have been published. I find one recent book is particularly good. *Adventure Cycling* by Tim Hughes (Blandford Press, 1978, hardback, 230 pp) contains a lot of sound advice about cycling in general, but with a strong touring content. Some other valuable books are described in the "Holidays" section, Chapter 8.

4. General literature

The Penguin Book of the Bicycle R. Watson and M. Grey (Penguin, 1978, 332 pp), is an anthology of the literature, history and purpose of the bicycle, very readable and worth keeping at hand for dipping into.

Cycling yearbooks have been tried and failed before, but *The International Cycling Guide* edited by Nick Crane (Tantivy Press, 1980 and annually, 288 pp) seems to have sold well, and should grow into an essential reference book. The main frustration about the first edition is that it lacks an index.

5. Cycling literature

Books describing particular races and touring experiences abound. My favourites in these two categories are *The Great Bike Race* by Geoffrey Nicholson (Magnum paperbacks, 1978, 75p) describing the 1976 Tour, and a quaint but very readable touring book, *A Man, A Bike, Alone Through Scotland* by Eugene Cantin (World Publications, £2.25). The description of Edinburgh bike shops should amuse Edinburgh readers.

Two well known fictional accounts of cycling are both humourous, although their humour is very different. *Three Men on the Bummel* by Jerome K. Jerome, is not as hilarious as the famous *Three Men in a Boat*. This account of a cycle trip through Germany in the 1930's has its moments.

The Third Policeman, by Flann O'Brien, is definitely an acquired taste in humour. The development of the theory concerning the transfer of personality between cyclist and machine is worth reading, even if you find the rest of the book impenetrable.

Appendices

APPENDIX I   CYCLING ORGANISATIONS

(a) OTHER LOCAL CYCLING ORGANISATIONS

Cyclists Touring Club

Founded 100 years ago by an Edinburgh medical student, the CTC has remained faithful to cycling and at present has over 40,000 members who cycle as a means of relaxation and exercise. As well as safeguarding cyclists' needs and rights, at national and local levels, the CTC arranges rides and tours in Britain and abroad and has some 300 local sections which provide a cycling and social programme all year round.

When you join the CTC you receive 12 months of personal service, friendly advice and practical help on all aspects of cycling, but, of course, it mainly attracts the serious cyclist who wishes the adventure of the open road 'away from it all'. The activities embrace: camping; rough stuff; Tourist Competitions; Medal Rides; Youth Hostel weekends; Bothy weekends; plus, if one desires, all the competitive side of racing.

Of particular value are the insurance and legal aid facilities which include free third party insurance cover up to £300,000. Routes, maps and practical advice on equipment and routes are available, and an illustrated magazine, 'Cycle Touring' is sent free to members every two months. There is also a good handbook with over 3,000 addresses of all the cyclists' needs. It is the largest and oldest cycling national cycling organisation with over 100 years' experience and gives 'pleasure locally and protection nationally'.

The recent history of the Lothians District Association of the CTC is one of continuing expansion and success. The 1970s have seen the membership grow from its lowest ever point in 1972 of 176 to its present figure of over 600, the highest ever. The DA is now the largest in Scotland. The DA also has its own country chalet. Further information may be obtained from the local secretary: **Mr. John D. Murdoch, 36 Comely Bank Place, Edinburgh EH4 1EP. Telephone: 031-332 5265.**

East of Scotland Cycling Association

To which the following 9 racing and touring clubs are affiliated. All fall into Lothian Region. The address given in usually the secretary's. Secretary: John Murdoch, 36 Comely Bank Place, Edinburgh EH4 1EP.

Bonnyrigg C.C. c/o R. J. Toole, 159 Newbattle Abbey Crescent, Eskbank, Midlothian.

Dunedin C.C. c/o R. J. Harris, 23 Barntongate Terrace, Edinburgh EH4 8BA. (Dunedin is the old name for Edinburgh).

Edinburgh Road Club Racing offshoot of the CTC. Successfully revived during 1970s. c/o John Murdoch, 36 Comely Bank Place, Edinburgh EH4 1EP.

Edinburgh University C.C. Also recently reformed, 2 years ago (after an absence of around 100 years). Now well established. Both touring and racing interests catered for (and frequent social events!). c/o Edinburgh University Sports Union, 46 The Pleasance, Edinburgh EH8 9TJ.

Livingston C.C. c/o J. McGraw, 28 Labrador Avenue, Howden, Livingston, West Lothian.

Lothians C.C. c/o J. Tighe, 14 Clermiston Crescent, Edinburgh.

Musselburgh Roads C.C. c/o Mrs. M. Lawson, 10 Sighthill Street, Edinburgh EH11 4QQ.

Rioseal Cycling Racing Team c/o Mrs. S.. Nisbet, 30 Newhaven Road, Edinburgh.

Velo Sportiv c/o J. B. Allan, 14/16 Jane Street, Leith, Edinburgh.

Another two Lothian Clubs have recently come to our notice:

Gorebridge Bike Club c/o Dorothy Watt, Brown Building, 80 Hinterfield Road, Gorebridge. EH23 4XA. Tel: Gorebridge 21808.

Wester Hailes Bike Group for rides, maintenance, campaigning etc. c/o Andrew Grant, Wester Hailes Education Centre, 5 Murrayburn Drive, Edinburgh EH14 2SU. Tel: 041-442 2201.

Finally **Friends of the Earth** run the **Community Bike Workshop** (See in Chapter 1). Further information from Richard Willis, 54 Findhorn Place, Edinburgh EH9 2NS. Telephone: 031-667 2543.

(b) OTHER CYCLING CAMPAIGN GROUPS IN SCOTLAND

Aberdeen Cyclists' Action Group, 2a St. Swithin Street, Aberdeen, or telephone Iain Brooker, Aberdeen 30306. Or call at 'Welly Boot' pub at 9 p.m. any Monday night.

Glasgow Cycling Campaign, 16 Newton Terrace, G3 2PJ. 041-221 6727

Inverness Cycling Campaign, c/o Mr. Thornton, 32a Castle Street, IV2 3DU.

Dumfries F.O.E. Cycle Section, c/o Mike Sale, Fishers Holt, Main Street, Penpont, Dumfries, 0848 30722.

(c) NATIONAL AND INTERNATIONAL CYCLING ORGANISATIONS

British Cycling Bureau. Publicity for all aspects of cycling, stickers, posters and information) Stanhope House, Stanhope Place, London W2 2HH.

Cyclists' Touring Club (National Headquarters), Cotterell House, 69 Meadrow, Godalming, Surrey GUZ 3HS (048-68 1684).

Cycle Campaign Groups Interim Secretariat, c/o Connie Wolfe: to improve co-operation and communication between cycling interests. Columbo Street Sports Centre, London, SE1 8DN. 01-928 7220.

Friends of the Earth National Bike Campaign, c/o Don Mathew, 9 Poland Street, London, W!V 3DG. Tel: 01-434 1684.

International Bicycle Network, PO Box 8194, Philadelphia, PA 19191, USA.

Freewheeling Magazine. Highly recommended, covers all aspects of cycling. 14 Picardy Place, EH1 3TJ.

APPENDIX II   OTHER RELEVANT ORGANISATIONS

(a) OTHER TRANSPORT ORGANISATIONS

Pedestrians Association, 1 Wandworth Road, London SW8 2LJ. 01-582 6878.

Scottish Association for Public Transport, 113 West Regent Street, Glasgow G2 2RU, or c/o Morris Bradley, 13 Cornwall Street, EH1 2EQ, 229-6854.

Royal Society for the Prevention of Accidents, 41 S.W. Thistle Street Lane, Edinburgh EH2 1EW. 226-6856.

Transport 2000, 40 James Street, London W1. 01-486 8523.

Transport and Road Research Laboratories, Old Wokingham Road, Berkshire RG11 6AU.

Railway Development Society, BM RDS, London, WIV 6XX. 01-405 0433.

(b) OTHER RELEVANT LOCAL ORGANISATIONS

Friends of the Earth, 2 Ainslie Place, Edinburgh EH3 6AR. 225-6906.

Cockburn Association, 15 North Bank Street, Edinburgh EH1 2LP. 225-5085.

Edinburgh Planning Aid, c/o Fiona Hutchison, 29 Ulster Gardens, Edinburgh EH8 7LL. 661-5904. Free expert advice for community organisations on planning matters.

Environmental Resources Centre, (ERC) Old Broughton School, McDonald Road, Edinburgh EH7 4NN. 557-2135. Organisation and equipment for volunteers, constructs walkways etc.

Scottish Sports Council, 1/3 St. Colme Street, Edinburgh EH3 6AA.

Scottish Health Education Unit, Woodburn House, Canaan Lane, Edinburgh EH10 4S.

Scottish Tourist Board, 23 Ravelston Terrace, Edinburgh EH4 3EF.

Scottish Youth Hostels Association, 161 Warrender Park Road, Edinburgh EH9 1DT.

APPENDIX III   POLITICAL CONTACTS
(a) M P.S.

Member of European Parliament

Ian M. Dalziel   Lothians
21 Greenhill Gardens
Edinburgh EH10 4BI

Members of Parliament for Lothian

Member	Constituency	Telephone
Robin F. Cook, M.P. The Mill, 9 Oak Lane Edinburgh EH12 6XH	Edinburgh Central	031-334 8329
Ronald Brown, M.P. 167 Pilton Avenue Edinburgh EH5 2HP	Edinburgh Leith	031-552 6824
Malcolm Rifkind M.P. 8 Old Church Lane Duddingston Village Edinburgh EH15 3PX	Edinburgh Pentlands	031-661 4716
Lord J. A. Douglas Hamilton, M.P. Lady Stairs Close Lawnmarket Edinburgh EH1 2NY	Edinburgh West	031-225 1482
Alex Eadie, M.P. Balkerack, The Haugh East Wemyss Fife KY1 4SB	Midlothian	Buckhaven 713636
Gavin S. Strang, M.P. 80 Argyle Crescent Edinburgh EH15 2QD	Edinburgh East	031-669 5999
A. M. Fletcher, C.A., M.P. 14 Cammo Walk Edinburgh EH4 8AN	Edinburgh North	031-556 5873
Michael Ancram, M.P. 6 Ainslie Place Edinburgh EH3 6AR	Edinburgh South	031-226 3147
John Home Robertson, M.P. Paxton South Mains Paxton, Berwickshire	Berwick and East Lothian	Paxton 86354
Tam Dalyell, M.P. The Binns, Linlithgow West Lothian EH49 7NA	West Lothian	Philpstoun 255

(b) LOTHIAN REGION COUNCILLORS Details as at September, 1980

To contact a councillor write to Lothian Region Chambers, Parliament Square, Edinburgh 1. For further details, such as which ward a particular street is in, phone the Department of Administration, Lothian Regional Council, 229 9292 Ext. 2049. The Bartholomews fold-out coloured city map (from newsagents) also has all city wards marked on it.

Key: COMMITTEES (* = group leader on committee)

1 = Planning & Development
2 = Policy & Resources
3 = Leisure Services
   a = Countryside Advisory
   b = Sports & Physical Recreation Advisory
   c = Tourism Advisory
4 = Transportation
   a = Highways subcommittee
   b = Transport subcommittee

BICYCLES

C = cyclist
R = attended SPOKES rally
M = SPOKES member
S = not member, but sympathetic

LABOUR (Convener = J. Crichton; Group Secretary - W. Taylor; Vice Convener - A. Bell) (TOTAL = 26)

Name	Ward	Phone	Committees/Bicycles
Bell, Alexander	Whitburn	Whit 40556	
Boyes, Peter	Mayfield/Gorebridge	660 1789	I
Buchanan, Mrs. Johan	Dalry/Tynecastle	669 3988	I
Burnett, James	Royston/Granton	661 8835	4a
Burns, Mrs. Jessie	Musselburgh	665 4198	3a
Cook, James	Pilrig/Calton	443 6811	2 3c 4b RS
Coyne, Michael	Broxburn	11 Freeland Av. Brxbn	3ac 4a
Crichton, John	Harbour/Connington	554 3201	2* S
Docherty, Michael	Dalkeith	663 1974	1* 2
Drummond, William	Armadale	Harthill 489	4b
Filsell, Mrs Catherine	Moat/Polwarth	445 2043	2 3 4*ab S
Hanlon, William	Livingston	Bathgate 53816	1 2
Herriot, Mrs. Phyllis	Willowbrae/Craigentinny	661 4304	2
Lindsay, Neil	Pilton/Muirhouse	332 0760	2 3
McNeill, George	Fa'side	Tranent 610292	2 3*abc
Milligan, Eric	Sighthill/Stenhouse	441 1528	2 4ab
Monies, Mrs. Madeleine	Links/Lorne	669 2875	1 2 S
Mulvey, John	Slateford/Hailes	661 7750	4b
Nisbet, James	Gladsmuir & Preston	Preston 812194	2 4b
Nolan, Paul	Niddrie/Craigmillar	Work: 661 5877	
Rankine, William	Calders	W. Calder 206	2 4b
Roe, William	Holyrood/Meadows	556 7170	1 4a CRM
Rogan, Mrs. Jess	Alnwickhill/Kaimes	667 8199	1 3b RS
Taylor, William	Lochrin/Tron	556 7170	2 3 CRM
Wilson, Peter	Inch/Gilmerton	667 2031	2 3
Young, John	Bonnyrigg/Newtongrange	663 8004	2

CONSERVATIVE (Leader = B. Meek; Group Secretary = J. Gilchrist) (TOTAL = 18)

Name	Ward	Phone	Committees/Bicycles
Berry, Ian	Portobello	669 4161	3bc 4a CR
Cowan, Charles	Currie/Ratho	449 4141	
Cramond, Ian	Dean/St. Andrews	556 3452	4b
Donaldson, Mrs. Winifred	Drylaw/Comely Bank	332 2351	
Gilchrist, James	Merchiston/Colinton	447 2368	3*b
Gray, George	Garleton	E. Linton 275	1
Hall, Norman	Traprain	0620 2108	1 4a C
Henderson, Norman	Duddingston/Milton	669 7610	4*ab C?
Huggins, Mrs. Astrid	Prestonfield/Mayfield	556 2720	1 3 CRS
Knox Robert	Murrayfield/Blackhall	332 3644	
Lester, Anthony	Churchill/Braid	552 1471	
Meek, Brian	Fairmilehead/Firrhill	229 9292(work)	3a
Nicholson, Alleyne	Trinity Newhaven	225 1574	1
Noble, Mrs. Marjorie	Penicuik	Penicuik 74184	3a
Percy, William	Broughton/Inverleith	556 1336	1*
Reid, Rev. Gordon	Sciennes/Marchmont	229 6104	
Theurer, George	Corstorphine/Drumbrae	556 7979	1
Thomson, John	Cramond/Barnton	334 6919	4b CR

SNP (Leader = W. Hardie) (TOTAL = 3)

Anderson, Christine	Linlithgow/Uphall	Linlighgow 3578		
Hardie, William	Queensferry/Kirkliston	331 1856		
Ramsay, David	Bathgate	Bathgate 630236	4a C?S	

LIBERAL (TOTAL = 1)

Gorrie, Donald	Craigsbank/Carrick Knowe	337 2077	3bc CRM	

INDEPENDENT (TOTAL = 1)

Stoddart, Jeff	Loanhead/Lasswade	440 0181	1	S

(c) EDINBURGH DISTRICT COUNCILLORS Details as at September, 1980

To contact a councillor, write to them at The City Chambers, High Street, Edinburgh 1; or phone their number below, or try The City Chambers at 225 2424.

To find out which ward a particular street is in, ask at The Central Library or phone The City Chambers (225 2424 Ext. 202). Unfortunately, there is not yet a map on sale with the new district boundaries, but a copy may be inspected at The City Chambers by first phoning the above extension.

KEY: COMMITTEES

6 = Policy and Resources
7 = Planning and Development
8 = Recreation
* = Party group leader on this committee

BICYCLES

C = cyclist
R = attended SPOKES rally
M = SPOKES member
S = not member, but sympathetic

CONSERVATIVE (Lord Provost = Tom Morgan; Group Leader = Cornelius Waugh) (TOTAL = 31)

Councillor	Ward	Home phone	Work phone	Coms.	Bikes
Alexander, Kenneth	40: Tollcross	339 1557	225 6338	7	—
Brereton, Ralph	23: Murrayfield	226 7382	26 7382	—	—
Cavayo, Stanley	45: Portobello	669 3263	—	6 7*	—
Clark, Alastair	50: Marchmont	225 8070	—	7 8	CM
Crombie, John	13: North West Corstorphine	339 4817	225 8494	6	—
Drummond-Young, Duncan	26: Stockbridge	225 7031	—	6	—
Ferguson, Kenneth	48: Morningside	445 3503	225 7422	7	CM
Jackson, Allan	17: Broughton	552 8453	—	6	—
Kean, Eric	49: Sciennes	667 2233	226 7284	7	—
Knox, Mrs. Moira	16: Blackhall	332 3644	—	7 8	—
Macfie, Mrs. Kathleen	22: South East Corstorphine	556 1896	—	7 8	CRM
Macfarlane, William	47: Merchiston	337 9929	332 2525 Ext. 13	6	—
Mackenzie, Mrs. Agnes	6: Parkgrove	336 1528	—	8	—
Mackintosh, Alastair	5: Cramond	554 3930	—	6 8*	—
Maclennan, Derrick	53: Colinton	447 4307	226 7361	7 8	—
Mansbridge, Mrs. Nansi	55: Braidburn	447 6837	—	—	—
Martin, Paul	30: Craigentinny	554 4878	—	8	—
McAlpine, Mrs. Margaret	11: Newhaven	552 4391	554 3211	6	—
McAra, Gordon	44: Mountcastle	556 6889	225 8494	7	wife is member
Meek, Brian	56: Fairmilehead	—	229 9292/ 2371	8	—
Metcalfe, Anthony	57: Alnwickhill	441 5853	229 6046	—	—
Morgan, Rt. Hon. Tom	24: Dean	441 3245	—	6*	—
Paterson, Mrs. Ruby	52: Mayfield	667 5354	—	7	—
Petherick, James	34: Longstone	443 2036	—	8	—
Powell, Ritchie	3: Balerno	449 4886	—	—	—
Pringle, Mrs. Sarah	25: New Town	556 4298	—	7	—
Ritchie, David	51: Prestonfield	667 4659	667 0891	6 8	—
Robertson, Mrs. Elizabeth	4: Baberton	449 2077	—	6 8	—
Sivewright, Roderick	18: Inverleith	664 0474	225 3843	—	—
Taylor, Harry	43: Willowbrae	661 4451	556 1876	6	—
Waugh, Cornelius	10: Trinity	554 1688	—	6 8	—

LABOUR (Group Leader = Ian Campbell; Group Chairman = John McKay) (TOTAL = 25)

Councillor	Ward	Home phone	Work phone	Coms.	Bike
Barton, Mrs. Gertrude	54: Firrhill	445 1180	—	8	S
Brown, David	61: Niddrie	669 7287	—	7	—
Cairns, Robert	41: St. Giles	229 9042	—	7	S
Campbell, John	59: Inch	447 4972	667 1081	6	—
Dalgleish, Robert	12: Fort	552 3316	332 2411/202		
Griffiths, Nigel	32: South Hailes	557 1157	661 5521	—	S
Hastie, James	20: Harbour	554 1965	—	7 8	—
Henderson, James	36: Stenhouse	444 1826	—	—	—
Hurley, Norma	38: Shandon	557 0366	225 9451	—	S
Imrie, Russell	28: Lochend	661 7011	—	6 7	—
Kerley, Richard	42: Holyrood	668 1326	228 6561	6	M
Lazarowicz, Mark	31: North Hailes	444 1661	225 4111	—	CRM
Lonie, Robert	60: Gilmerton	664 4052	—	7	—
Mackenzie, Mrs. Bjorg	58: Haimes	664 1293	—	—	—
Mackenzie, Mrs. Eliz.	37: Dalry	554 8623	—	6	S
McKay, John	33: Sighthill	445 2865	—	8	—
McKinnon, Christopher	27: Calton	552 4878	556 2440/94	8	S
McLaughlin, Mrs. Eleanor	8: Muirhouse	445 4052	—	6	—
Monies, George	9: Granton	669 2875	443 6061	6 8	—
Nisbet, Thomas	29: Links	332 8313	—	8	—
Oliver, Mrs. Violet	46: Milton	669 9840	—	—	—
Saren, Michael	19: Lorne	337 8321	—	—	—
Wilson, John	35: Moat	664 9387	—	—	—
Wood, Alexander	7: Pilton	557 2902	—	6	S
Woodward, Val	39: Haymarket	228 6142	663 3700/ 1575	7	CRM

LIBERAL (TOTAL = 2)

Gorrie, Donald	21: South West Corstorphine	337 2077	225 8965	—	CRM
King, Derek	15: Telford	343 1801	667 1011 Ext. 6531	—	S

SNP (TOTAL = 2)

Irons, Norman	14: North East Corstorphine	337 6154	225 8455	—	—
Williams, Derek	2: Kirkliston	333 3655	333 3210	6 8	—

INDEPENDENT (TOTAL = 2)

Black, Mrs. Winnie	62: Craigmillar	669 7602	—	7	—
Milne, James	1: Queensferry	331 1329	—	7 8	—

Please write to your M.P. or councillor on any aspect you feel strongly about. For information on how to write to an official see SPOKES FACTS No. 3.

(d) LOCAL POLITICAL PARTIES

Communist Party 137 Buccleuch Street, EH8 9NE — Tel: 667 8383
Conservative Party 11 Atholl Crescent, EH3 8HA — 229 1342
Ecology Party 45 Niddry Street, EH1 1LG
Labour Party Ruskin House, 15 Windsor Street, EH7 5LA — 556 5158
or **Labour Transport Working Group** Pip Hills, 10 Scotland Street, EH3 6PS
Liberal Party 2 Atholl Place, EH3 8HP
Scottish National Party 6 N. Charlotte Street, EH2 4HR.